The REALM of the Reign

Reflections on ~~the~~ ~~Dominion o~~f God

Ben ~~Witherington III~~

DISCIPLESHIP RESOURCES

P.O. BOX 840 • NASHVILLE, TENNESSEE 37202-0840

www.discipleshipresources.org

Dedication

This book is dedicated to the members of the New Covenant adult Sunday school class of Centenary United Methodist Church in Lexington, Kentucky, where I have seen the dominion of God at work in a variety of wonderful ways. May God help us all to continue to be an expectant people, praying earnestly, "Thy Kingdom come."

Cover and book design by Sharon Anderson

Cover illustration: © Peter Pearson

Cover photo: © Telegraph Colour Library/FPG International LLC

ISBN 0-88177-249-6

Library of Congress Catalog Card No. 98-70469

DR249

Contents

Whatever Happened to Kingdomtide?

It was October, and there was something strange about the worship bulletin. At the top it read: "Twentieth Week After Pentecost." Suddenly it dawned on me that we had skipped a whole liturgical season of the church year! Now, if we had been following the Jewish liturgical calendar, this would have been quite unthinkable. Everyone knows that in the early fall after Pentecost (the Feast of Weeks) one looks forward to Rosh Hashanah, the Jewish New Year. But because the church has followed the Roman calendar, with the New Year celebrated after the winter solstice, we have no similar event in September or October.

What United Methodists are in fact *supposed* to be celebrating in the early fall is Kingdomtide. This is easily the most neglected season of the church year. One wonders why this is the case. Perhaps it is because we are not at all sure what the "Kingdom" is or how it differs from the church or from Israel; thus we are not sure what it is we are supposed to be celebrating. It is hoped that this study will provide a partial remedy for this problem as we explore together the "realm of God's reign."

Kingdomtide, 1998

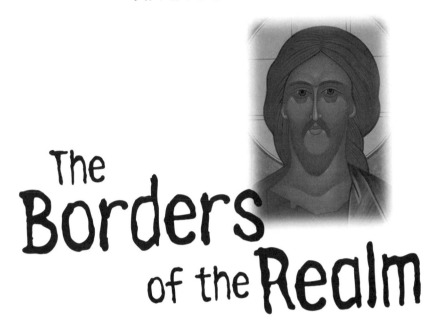

The Borders of the Realm

Mention the word *Kingdomtide* in the church today and you are likely to get quizzical looks. The same often can be said if you casually refer to the *kingdom of God*. There are several reasons for this puzzlement: The kingdom of God is an oft-neglected subject in Christian preaching and teaching; moreover, in many parts of the church, interest in things eschatological (teaching about the "end times") is waning.

Yet as we approach the millennium there has been an increased interest, even among the general public, in what shape our future will take. Both Kingdomtide as a season and Kingdom teaching have a good deal to say about the future of humanity and of the planet. It seems an appropriate time, then, for a book like this one to explore these matters.

Terms of Endowment

The appropriate place to begin our discussion is with defini-
tions, and here already we have a two-fold problem. The
first of our problems is historical. It was the famous French New
Testament scholar Alfred Loisy who once said words to the
effect that while Jesus preached the coming of the Kingdom, it
was the church that showed up. Does this mean—and here's the
theological problem—that the Kingdom has not yet come, or
that it came in a form that Jesus did not expect, namely, as the
church? This historical-theological problem can perhaps be
resolved if we look more directly at the difficulties of defining
terms such as *kingdom* and *church*.

To most modern people the term *kingdom* always implies a
place, whether one is thinking of the United Kingdom or the
Magic Kingdom. Yet the Greek term that we often translate
"kingdom" (*basileia*) and, more important, the Aramaic term that
Jesus likely used (*malkuta*) do not always refer to a place; in
fact, sometimes these terms do not refer to a place at all. At
times *basileia* and *malkuta* refer to an activity; at other times, to
a condition; and at still other times, to a place.

To be more specific, when the Greek or Aramaic word for
kingdom is used in conjunction with *God*, the term sometimes
refers to God's saving activity, sometimes to the resulting condition of that activity in someone's life (namely God's rule in one's
life), and sometimes to a place one enters, inherits, obtains, or is
excluded from at the end of human history. In all cases, the
term *kingdom of God* refers to something that is part of God's
final design or plan for humankind—namely, salvation.

I would suggest that we use the word *dominion* instead of
kingdom. The reason for this is that the English word *dominion* can refer to an activity (God exercises or has dominion
over us, and we are in turn ruled by God) or a place (God's
dominion is the place where the divine rule is manifested).
Dominion also expresses better the intent of the title of this

book: *Realm* is meant to indicate both the spatial dimension and the active influence of God's reign.

Lest all this sounds like an exercise in theological abstractions and semantics, we need to remind ourselves that the dominion of God rather than the church was the featured subject of all Jesus' parables, as well as much of early Christian preaching. It is thus important for us to get a clear grip on the meaning and importance of this language.

One conclusion will become very apparent as we move along: Jesus and his followers believed that there was an *already* and a *not-yet* dimension to this dominion. For Jesus and the disciples this meant that they saw themselves as witnesses and heralds—even bringers—of the final (or "end-time") dominion of God into the world. In their view, the future was *now*. Jesus put the matter this way: "But if it is by the finger of God that I cast out the demons, then the kingdom [dominion] of God has come to you" (Luke 11:20; see also Matthew 12:28). The coming of the Dominion was signaled by the miracles of Jesus and their interpretation by Jesus.

From what we have said, it will be apparent that Kingdomtide is the celebration of God's final saving activity, breaking into our midst and leading us on until "thy kingdom come, thy will be done, on earth as it is in heaven" (Matthew 6:10, Revised Standard Version). It is appropriate that this celebration takes place in the fall, for images of bringing in the harvest or celebrating the harvest with thanksgiving are an integral part to this church season. Joy and gratitude, excitement and a sense of fulfillment, are the emotions of and reactions to Kingdomtide.

But until the Lord returns, the celebration of the dominion of God will always be an already and not-yet affair. It is rather like the sort of celebration that takes place on a wedding day. For the couple involved, once the wedding service has been completed, the marriage is a present reality; therefore, celebration is already in order. Yet there is still in front of them the consummation of the marriage and, it is hoped, a lifetime of happy union together; hence, their marriage is not yet completed.

Similarly, the church awaits the consummation of her relationship with the Lord when he returns, but there is already reason to celebrate. God's saving activity has already transpired in our midst: God has created a people, based on a real and recognized union between the Bridegroom and the bride.

The already and not-yet dimensions of the dominion of God and of our relationship with God must be kept steadily in view throughout this study. To those who think we have already been blessed with all that a relationship with God can mean, we will have to say, "Not yet." But to those who think God's dominion has to do only with "pie in the sky by and by," we must say, "Already!"

Israel, Church, Dominion

Church folk are apt to mistake the Dominion for the church. A moment's reflection will show, however, that the two terms do not refer to exactly the same entity. For one thing, we are not praying for the church to come; but every time we say the Lord's Prayer, we ask God to send God's dominion. For another thing, we don't talk about obtaining or inheriting the church, but we certainly use these terms in talking about God's dominion. Nevertheless, it is right to say that God's dominion can be seen within the church—if by "church" we mean the people of God. There is a sense in which—as God rules, saves, and transforms God's people so that they become the dominion of God—the church is at least the *place* where that dominion can be seen and experienced.

By the same token, Israel and God's dominion should not be identified with each other either. If by "dominion" we mean God's rule among God's people, then *wherever* God's people can be found, there also is the Dominion. Doubtless, Ezekiel was surprised to have his vision of the chariot and the throne while swatting mosquitoes at the Chebar River in Babylon

(Ezekiel 1-2); however, it was intended as a reminder that God and the divine presence and activity were not confined to Mount Zion in Jerusalem, or even to the land of Israel. Furthermore, as the story of Jonah teaches us, God was prepared to accept followers even from among the Ninevites if they repented and honored the one true God (Jonah 4:11). There are also warnings that God's ruling presence can be withdrawn from a group of God's people if they are faithless (Matthew 21:43; Romans 11). On the other hand, as we shall see, it is clear that Jesus and his earliest followers did expect the final manifestation of God's dominion on earth to have the land of Israel and the risen patriarchs in that land as its focus (Matthew 19:28; Luke 13:28).

The relationship between the church and Israel is more complicated. On the one hand, all of Jesus' earliest followers were Jews—as, of course, was Jesus himself. Furthermore, after Easter and Pentecost, as far as we can tell from a close reading of Acts 1–4, all the Christians who made up the Jerusalem church were also Jews. There was, then, a time when the church was a subset of Judaism, which took many different forms in the first century C.E. (Common Era).

However, it appears equally clear that most non-Christian Jews came to view Christians as not true Jews, due principally to Christians' belief in and worship of Jesus. To complicate matters further, the earliest Jewish Christians saw themselves as the very definition of true Jews. By the time we get to what is probably Paul's earliest extant letters—Galatians and 1 and 2 Thessalonians, all written somewhere around 50 C.E.—a clear distinction is made between Jews, on the one hand, and the followers of Jesus, on the other. Even more strikingly, Paul applies to the church language previously reserved only for Israel. At one point he even calls Jews and Gentiles who are united in Christ—or at least Jewish Christians—"the Israel of God" (Galatians 6:16).

Finally, if we read Romans 9–11 carefully, it will become apparent that Paul believes three things: First, God has not cast off God's first chosen people or reneged on God's promises to them. Second, those who have rejected Christ or are outside of Christ have been temporarily separated from the people of God. That means that not all Jews are true Jews. For now, Paul affirms, a true Jew is one who recognizes Jesus as the Jewish Messiah, as Paul and the apostles had done. Third, when the full number of Gentiles have become part of the people of God, Christ will return and "all Israel [that is, those not already Christians] will be saved" (Romans 11:26). By this Paul seems to mean that a very large number of Jews who hitherto had not believed in Christ will be saved.

The upshot of this somewhat complicated discussion is that, as in the case of the church, Israel cannot simply be equated with the dominion of God. Nor should we assume that in the New Testament the term *Israel* always refers to the church. The fact is, in some instances the term *Israel* refers to Jews and Gentiles united in Christ, while in other cases it refers to non-Christian Jews.

It is not surprising that we sometimes get confused about the relationship between God's dominion, the church, and Israel. What is crucial to bear in mind is that God's dominion has a wider meaning than either of the concepts *church* or *Israel* on their own. God's saving activity can happen outside the Jewish and the Christian communities; indeed, this is what missionary work accomplishes. Needless to say, it can happen outside the nation of Israel or of the United States of America; in fact, God's saving work can happen outside any of the nations that have traditionally had a Judeo-Christian heritage. Furthermore, God's redemptive activity can break into our midst quite apart from our prayers or plans. God and the divine activity cannot be confined or domesticated by God's people. The New Testament reminds us, however, that God has *chosen* to activate and implement God's eschatological dominion through one specific person and his activities: Jesus Christ. We will say much more on this subject later.

Thus at Kingdomtide we are celebrating the great saving acts of God throughout salvation history, but especially those acts that began with the coming of Jesus. This divine activity, which resulted in a gathered people of God, is cause for celebration not least because it reminds us that God and the divine plan is larger than we could ever imagine. God's plan cannot be confined to a particular time of year, a particular denomination, a particular church, a particular country, or even a particular age.

Since the coming of Christ, the world has indeed been living in the eschatological age during which God's final saving blessings are available already, at least in part. The end times are not merely near; they are already here, ever since the Messiah came to earth. Yet there is never a time when the Dominion is so fully present that we do not need to continue to pray, "Thy kingdom come, thy will be done, on earth as it is in heaven." God's dominion, or reign, is at present perfectly manifested only in heaven, which is also God's realm. While God's reign is manifested from place to place and from time to time on earth now, no one can point to a full manifestation of that dominion on earth. It is the full manifestation of God's reign to which Christians look forward when they reflect on the meaning of Kingdomtide and pray, "Thy kingdom come."

Our task in this book is to unpack more fully some of the issues discussed above and to develop their implications for the church today. The study is divided into two main parts, each consisting of several chapters. Part One, titled "The Powerful Presence," focuses on the reality of God's dominion as it manifests itself in the present day. This is the "already" aspect of the Dominion. Part Two, titled "The Glorious Future," deals, not surprisingly, with the "not-yet" aspect of God's dominion—the aspect that lies ahead of us and is as yet unrealized.

It is my hope that this study will spark an ongoing exploration of the importance of the dominion of God for the church and for the individual Christian. I also hope that it will help us to see the validity and, indeed, the importance of celebrating this reality in Kingdomtide.

For now, for those of us who live in the in-between time— in the time between the first and second coming of Christ—the watchword for God's dominion on earth must be *already,* but also *not yet.*

Questions for Reflection

1 Why does this book prefer the term *dominion* to *kingdom* in speaking of God's saving activity on earth?

2 Before reading this chapter, had you ever heard of Kingdomtide? Why, do you suppose, is Kingdomtide the most neglected season of the church year?

3 How does the relationship between the Dominion, the church, and Israel help you understand how and where God's dominion may be manifested on earth?

Part One

The
Powerful
Presence

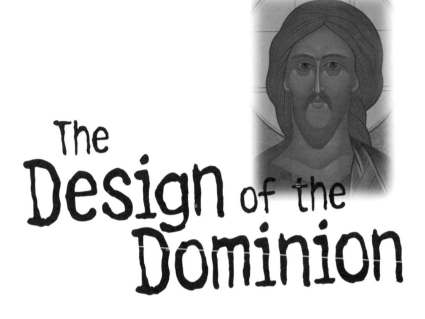

CHAPTER ONE

The Design of the Dominion

I n this first chapter we deal with the *manner* in which the dominion of God has come into human lives since Jesus first walked among us. As we shall see, the heart of the matter is a matter of the heart. That is, God's design is to begin the renewal of the world by recreating human beings in the divine image—by saving and transforming human lives, one life at a time. God accomplishes this design not in the abstract but rather concretely through Jesus Christ. Christ was the embodiment of God's dominion on earth. And it is as we are conformed to Christ's image through God's saving activity in us that we become "Christ-bearers" and "Dominion-bearers" to others.

The Evidence of the Dominion

At one point in Luke's presentation of Jesus' teaching, the Pharisees ask Jesus when the dominion of God is coming. Jesus responds: "The kingdom [dominion] of God is not coming with things that can be observed; nor will they say, 'Look, here it is!' or 'There it is!' For, in fact, the kingdom [dominion] of God is among you" (Luke 17:20-21). The question of the Pharisees is quite understandable. They expected clear visible signs or evidence of the Dominion's coming—signs such as the resurrection of the righteous, the appearance of a messianic figure that would cast Israel's enemies out of the land, and the renewal of the land of Israel itself. Jesus is suggesting that the Dominion is *already* present—in his ministry.

But the visible signs of the Dominion's presence are not what people expected or were told. Indeed, the only visible sign of the Dominion during Jesus' ministry was the evidence of changed human lives—that is, the evidence of the impact that Jesus' words and miraculous deeds had on those who encountered him. This is very much the manner in which the Dominion is present today. Lives are still being changed by the proclamation and application of the good news, but the fallen world as we know it continues without any other visible signs of transformation.

Luke 17:20-21 raises important issues about when and how God's reign is present on earth. For example, when Christians around the world pray daily, "Thy kingdom come, thy will be done, on earth...," does this not imply that the Dominion has largely *not* come on earth? Does this not suggest that God's plan—God's design—for humankind has failed to be fully implemented in the first two thousand years of church history? Is this not precisely why so many church people are wary of the end-time predictions and promises made by zealous fundamentalist evangelists?

One thing that these prophets of imminent doom and the end of the world have had in common through the ages is that they have all had a perfect track record: They have all been wrong. Does this then mean that Alfred Loisy was right when he said that the Kingdom has not come, and that, instead, only the church has shown up?

These are difficult questions, and it is not hard to understand why some Christians, as well as most non-believers, have tuned out apocalyptic (end-time) prophets and preachers and ignored or repudiated, or tried to transform, the eschatological language of the New Testament into a more palatable form of discourse. Yet those who do so have clearly missed the point of Luke 17:20-21. In this text, Jesus was warning us that the coming of God's dominion on earth would not be accompanied by dramatic signs in the sky, or evidence of the end of the world. To the contrary—and no doubt to the shock of the Pharisees—Jesus was saying that the Dominion was *already* in their midst and that they were missing it! But what exactly was it that they were missing?

Like millions of people today, the Pharisees were overlooking the essence of the divine design—namely, that God sets up the Dominion in the lives of those who receive God. This is what Christians today mean when they say that Christ "rules in their hearts" or is "Lord of their lives." The reign of God has come to the most personal of locations: the inner life of individual human beings, and the community of God's people.

The Heart of the Dominion

For some people, the notion that the dominion of God is manifested in the human heart will seem unnecessarily restrictive: For them, the heart is far too small and cramped a space for God to work, especially if God's saving activity is going to make a difference in the world. For others, focusing on the heart as the place where the Dominion comes is to over-spiritualize the concept of God's dominion. Are we being too heavenly minded to be of any earthly good?

While such reactions are understandable, they fail to come to grips with the fact that most of the major problems human beings face in life originate in the human heart. Take war, murder, adultery, drug addiction, theft, idolatry, or racist and sexist acts— all of these horrors ultimately begin in the human heart. Jesus understood this, and at one point condemned the lusts of the heart (Matthew 5:27-28). God's saving dominion comes to deal with the *source* of social maladies—the human heart—not simply to deal with the effects or communal expressions of such maladies (though responding to these is also important).

Once when discussing the issue of clean and unclean food, Jesus remarked:

> Do you not see that whatever goes into a person from outside cannot defile, since it enters, not the heart but the stomach?... It is what comes out of a person that defiles. For it is from within, from the human heart, that evil intentions come: fornication, theft, murder, adultery, avarice, wickedness, deceit, licentiousness, envy, slander, pride, folly.
>
> (Mark 7:18-22)

In Jesus' view, the heart was the heart of the matter: Humankind desperately needs a "heart transplant," not merely a "heart bypass."

In both the Old and the New Testaments, the human heart is seen as the "control center" of human personality. It is the place where one finds the person's thoughts, emotions, and will. This is why in the Bible we read, for instance, about the "thoughts of the heart." God knew that if the control center of the human personality could be taken hold of and pointed in the right direction, the rest of the person would follow. It is like leading a horse to water: If the horse wears a halter and one can get hold of it and turn the horse's head, the rest of the horse will follow. So too with human beings. Once God gets hold of a person's heart, the renovation of the whole person has been set in motion. When the heart is led in a particular direction, the rest will follow.

If I still haven't convinced you of the importance of God's reign in the human heart, consider the following illustrations: Take the recent laudable campaign against drugs in public schools. The campaign slogan is "Just say no." The assumption behind the campaign is that young people will have the power to reject drugs if they are better informed and sufficiently exhorted. The problem with this assumption is that information without inner transformation will not, and cannot, finally solve the problem of drug abuse. *The human heart must be changed if people are to be really different.* A new attitude, not just new ideas, is required. If we really want to end the drug problem in the United States of America, we would do well not merely to *preach* but also to *pray* that God's transforming, saving activity might break into the lives of the thousands of troubled people who are addicted to one kind of drug or another.

Take another example: Recently I had occasion to see a powerful play titled *God's Country,* which was written by Steven Dietz (Samuel French, Inc., 1990). The play deals with the problem of racism in society. It shows how racism can lead a group of people to assume that they are normal while all others who are not like them are strange or suspicious, even wicked. Dietz drives home the point that racism originates in the human heart; and more to the point, racism is based on and driven by the irrational fears and illogical assumptions that often reside in the heart.

It is precisely because human beings are fallen creatures and their thoughts and feelings are often dark and dangerous that God's dominion must first invade and take over the human heart, if human society is to be improved. Jesus understood this fact; therefore, he proclaimed the Dominion in a way that helped people realize that when God comes to dwell in fullness within them, God demands—and delivers—a change in their lives. This change leads not just to the power of positive thinking but to a transformed will and healed emotions.

Of course, my insistence on this point of God's saving presence in human lives is based on the presupposition that human beings are not all right in their present condition. That is to say, human beings are fallen and cannot get up by their own efforts. They are lost in a world of self-centered and self-seeking ventures; and they require a radical rescue operation to be set right so they can learn to truly love others—to become *other*-centered. When the dominion of God enters our hearts, it takes us out of the circus-like hall-of-mirrors environment in which we perpetually look at and admire various configurations of ourselves. Instead, it places us in the presence of God, from whose vantage point we can see the world as it really is and understand our own place in it.

The evidence that God is working in the believer's life will be manifested in his or her relationships with fellow Christians and with the world. The apostle Paul says: "For the kingdom [dominion] of God is not food and drink but righteousness and peace and joy in the Holy Spirit" (Romans 14:17). Righteousness, peace, and joy—qualities the Spirit forms in the life of the believer—are evidence that God's saving activity is at work in the person's life. They are evidence that the Holy Spirit has taken up residence in the person. The starting point, however, is the transformed inner life of the individual.

The Will of the Dominion

Our discussion thus far raises some important questions about God's will for humankind. It raises questions about what might be God's plan—God's design—for human lives. In the broad sense, these questions are easy to answer. God desires that all people be saved, that all be conformed to the image of Jesus, that all, in short, become their best selves. Paul states the matter succinctly: "For this is the will of God, your sanctification..." (1 Thessalonians 4:3). God is a holy and loving God and desires to create a holy and loving people. This is what it means to adequately reflect God's image on earth. When God's character is reflected in our character and in our daily lives, then the dominion of God is evident on earth. Then God's will is being done on earth as it is already in heaven.

If the dominion of God in the present is chiefly about our becoming holy people, many of us may be dismayed by how far short of God's holiness we fall. This reaction is both understandable and proper. We do sin and fall short of God's best for our lives. But we need to understand that salvation, God's saving activity in our lives, is a matter of grace; it is not something we earn. This is why Jesus reassures his followers by saying: "Do not be afraid, little flock, for it is the Father's good pleasure to give you the kingdom [dominion]" (Luke 12:32). The Dominion comes into our lives as a gift, not as something we have earned; and its effects, including holiness, are likewise a gift. Yet, once God's dominion has been given to us, it requires our all in order to manifest it and live it out: "No one who puts a hand to the plow and looks back is fit for the kingdom [dominion] of God" (Luke 9:62).

The gift and responsibility to be "Dominion-bearers" accords with God's design that the Dominion come to pass concretely, through and in the lives of people. God's design took on concrete form in Jesus Christ. Indeed, Jesus was not just the *revelation* of God's will on earth but also the concrete *implementation* of that will. Jesus embodied the will of God and delivered God's saving presence to others.

Similarly, Christians embody the dominion of God for others by reflecting the character of Christ in what they say and do. Through our words and our actions, through our attempts to live out the gift of holiness, others can be saved, can come to have a relationship with Christ as Lord of their lives. In this way, the Dominion came and continues to come, first through Jesus and then through those who are in Christ—the "Christ-bearers."

The Hope of the Dominion

We live in a world that, after two world wars in this century and various lesser conflicts, has a rather jaded view about the future. In fact, many people, including many of our young people, could be called people without hope. The flip side of this loss of hope is a sort of *carpe-diem* (or "seize-the-moment") approach to life. One hears this attitude in slogans such as "He who hesitates is lost" or "The early bird gets the worm."

In light of this kind of tunnel vision or fixation on the present moment, some people have thought that the only solution for such a narrow field of focus is to speak in dramatic or shocking or winsome ways about the future so as to jolt people out of their narcissism. Jesus would not have entirely agreed with this logic.

To be sure, parts of Jesus' message to his own people—many of whom had abandoned hope because of the crushing tyranny of Roman rule—had a future dimension to it. The dominion of God was not fully present, and so Jesus taught his disciples to pray: "Thy kingdom come...". But at the same time, as we have noticed thus far, both Jesus and Paul were also saying: "The future is *now*." Already God's saving activity was breaking into the midst of Jesus' disciples. Already human lives were being changed and a new community of believers formed. Already the sick were being healed; already the blind were gaining sight; already the lost were being found. Jesus did not come just to *announce* the coming of God's saving reign upon the earth; he came to *inaugurate* it.

When Columbus approached King Ferdinand and Queen Isabella about finding a new passage to the Orient, the motto on the Spanish flag was *Ne plus ultra*, which means "There is nothing beyond"—in this case, nothing beyond the realm of the Spanish Empire. Yet in 1492, without looking for it, Columbus discovered the New World. Thereafter it became apparent that the motto of the Empire needed to be changed. It should read: *Plus ultra,* which means "There *is* more beyond."

In a sense, *plus ultra* captivates the message of the Gospels, especially texts such as Luke 17:20-21. In texts such as these, Jesus is saying: "There is more in your midst than meets the eye; there is more beyond what is empirically evident." There is visible evidence for God's in-breaking dominion—evidence manifested only through changed human lives.

However, we should also remember that what God is doing now in our lives is but a foretaste of things to come, a preview of "coming attractions." To the thief on the cross who asked to be remembered when Jesus came into his dominion, Jesus replied: "Truly I tell you, today you will be with me in Paradise" (Luke 23:43). It is interesting that in Luke's Gospel, these are Jesus' last words to another human being before his death. The Dominion was on Jesus' mind right to the end; and he believed it had a future, however glorious some of the present manifestations of the Dominion might have been. Jesus' motto was *plus ultra*: There is more beyond.

Conclusion

For a jaundiced world, which thinks there is nothing new under the sun and nothing to look forward to in life, the gospel of God's dominion offers a rebuttal. It suggests that there is grace here and glory hereafter, if one will set one's eyes on God's dominion rather than on human realms and reigns.

Adoniram Judson, the famous missionary to Burma, was right when he told a tribal chieftain, even as the latter was about to kill Judson, that the future was as bright as God's promises. Jesus said as much when he reassured us that it is God's will and design to give us the dominion of God—in part now, in full later.

Christians have often been accused of peddling a message of "pie in the sky by and by." But what we have learned in this chapter is that the dominion of God—the saving activity of God, the reign of God in human lives—is *already* happening in our midst through the work of Jesus and the Holy Spirit. Therefore, God has a track record. We look forward to the future based on what we know God has already accomplished for us in the past. In Christ we have been saved, we are being saved, and we shall be saved.

In the next chapter, we raise more specific questions about God's dominion. We said that the earth is the place where God's reign becomes manifest. We also learned that the evidence for God's dominion on earth is seen chiefly in transformed human lives. But what is the place and role of the church in God's dominion? To this question we turn in Chapter Two.

Questions for Reflection

1 How is a person's life different when God begins to reign—becomes Lord—in his or her life?

2 What is God's will for humanity? for the earth?

3 What is Jesus' role in implementing the coming of God's dominion?

4 Why is the human heart the target of God's design for the Dominion? How do changed hearts help change the world?

5 What does the prayer "Thy kingdom come" tell us about the *present* dimensions of God's saving activity? What does it say about the *future* of God's dominion?

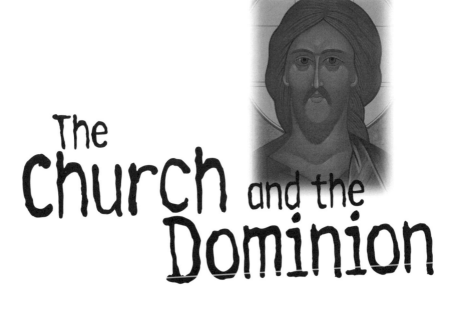

CHAPTER TWO

The Church and the Dominion

T hus far we have considered the definition, nature, and location of God's dominion on earth and how it is manifested in human lives. Building on these insights we now ask: What is the relationship of the *church* to the manifestation of God's dominion on earth? In what ways can the church better manifest that dominion? Furthermore, what is the difference between a church that has a "domination mentality" and a church that manifests the Dominion? These are the issues we will address in this chapter.

The Place of the Church in the Dominion

In thinking about the relationship between the church and God's dominion, it helps to keep in mind that the Dominion cannot be limited to a specific locale such as the Holy Land (or, for that matter, any other geographical location). As we saw in the previous chapter, the Dominion is found wherever God's transforming Spirit is at work. For Paul and Jesus both, the saving work of God happens through the proclaiming of the good news and through acts of help and healing performed by the followers of Jesus in his name.

Of course this means that God's dominion is indeed found within the context of God's people, the church. There preeminently one would expect to find the good news proclaimed and lives being saved, helped, and healed. But as we saw, it is a mistake to identify God's dominion simply with the church. To be sure, God's saving activity happens among the people of God; but it also happens when missionaries go to places where the gospel has not been shared before.

Jesus was not prepared to identify Israel in his day with God's dominion; rather, he sought to bring the Dominion *into* the midst of Israel so that Israel could be redeemed. Likewise, God's dominion does break into the context of the gathered community of Christians, but it also enters the places where Christians scatter for service and ministry.

The Church as the Manifestation of the Dominion

How, then, does the church manifest the evidence that God rules its life, that God has transformed this particular group of people? The answer to this question is complex. First, we can point to corporate worship as a clear sign that a particular group of people recognizes the sovereignty of God. In worship, we believers acknowledge that God is the ruler of the universe and that we are not. In other words, we recognize God as God, and ourselves as God's creatures—and thus less than

God. True worship makes clear the distinction between Creator and creature. We humans should not be seen as objects of worship; only God—Father, Son, and Holy Spirit—deserves to be worshiped and thus recognized as Sovereign of the universe. Authentic worship is the opposite of idolatry, which by definition is the act of worshiping as God someone or something that is less than and other than God.

Second, the church manifests the evidence of God in its midst by displaying—both in the lives of Christian individuals and in its life together as a group—the qualities that are the result of God's presence: love, joy, peace, patience, kindness, goodness, self-control, righteousness, holiness, and many more. Basically, when one sees the character of God in Christ in a person's or a group's life, one witnesses the evidence of God's dominion in that person or group. But these qualities are not displayed in the abstract; rather, they are traits that reveal themselves in concrete works of piety and charity.

When we think of works of piety, we think, for instance, of *prayer*, which is a clear sign that a person is seeking the help of a higher power and is thus trying to align him or herself properly with the will of God. *Confession,* too, is a proper work of piety manifesting the dominion of God. For example, Paul says that a person transformed by Christ's saving activity will confess with the lips that Jesus is Lord and believe in the heart that God raised Jesus from the dead (Romans 10:9). Such a person is manifesting the rule or dominion of God in his or her life.

But it is not just by acts of devotion that a believer manifests the Dominion in his or her life. In 1 John 3:24, we read that all who obey God's commandments (*obey* here refers specifically to believing in Jesus and loving one another) abide in God, and God abides in them. *Obedience* to God's Word is a sign of the presence of God's reign in a person's life. Notice, too, that the opposite of obedience is taken as a clear sign that one has not experienced God's rule or saving activity in one's life. Consider

Paul's warning: "Do you not know that wrongdoers will not inherit the kingdom [dominion] of God? Do not be deceived! Fornicators, idolaters, adulterers, male prostitutes, sodomites, thieves, the greedy, drunkards, revilers, robbers—none of these will inherit the kingdom [dominion] of God" (1 Corinthians 6:9-10). In these verses, Paul is speaking about the future dimension of God's dominion, when it fully comes on earth. But the point is that indulging in such sinful patterns of behavior now can lead to eventual exclusion from the Dominion. In this passage, Paul is clearly reckoning with the possibility that Christians can and do sin against God's saving presence in their lives— hence his warning. Paul's concern is that such sinful behavior, *if persisted in*, could lead to exclusion from God's presence and dominion in the end.

God's dominion on earth may also be seen in deeds of charity—whether deeds of righteousness or deeds of love. Obviously, the primary deed of love the church can do for a fallen world is to share the gospel with it. The early church understood clearly that God's dominion is spread through evangelism and the work of missions. But there are other valid ministries of love also: helping the poor or the sick (Mother Teresa spent her life doing this), building houses for Habitat for Humanity, collecting funds for famine relief, or supporting a child through the Christian Children's Fund.

It is important to stress, however, that God's dominion is also evidenced through deeds of righteousness. Here the church can play a crucial role. Deeds of righteousness include opposing racism or sexism, working for fairness and equality in the workplace, seeking to reform the justice system to make it more equitable, or ensuring that the powerless and those with disabilities in our society are taken care of by working for tax reform.

One recent example of a deed of righteousness involves Methodist Bishop Peter Storey. Along with Bishop Desmond Tutu and others, Bishop Storey opposed apartheid in South Africa by nonviolent means until the system was abolished. He told me many moving stories of the cost of discipleship in that situation, the cost of manifesting God's dominion on earth. Bishop Storey's son faced imprisonment for refusing to serve in the South-African military, which enforced the system of apartheid. On various occasions, the bishop himself faced down the guns in order to protect others.

In a fallen world, the dominion of God will always be opposed by the powers of darkness, and real transformation in society often comes slowly and painfully. The experiences of Bishop Storey and others show that it is not enough for God to reign in the human heart; the Dominion must also manifest itself in our everyday behavior, our relationships, our society. God demands of the church a bold witness *for* Christ and a prophetic witness *against* evil and injustice.

The Dominion and the Church's Mandate to Improve

What can the church do to be a place where God's dominion is always manifested more and more faithfully? Several possibilities come to mind. First, the church must seek to be a fellowship of *the transformed.* That means that it must manifest the character of God both within its own fellowship and in its dealings with the world. First John 4:20 is quite clear on this point: "Those who say, 'I love God,' and hate their brothers and sisters, are liars; for those who do not love a brother or sister whom they have seen, cannot love God whom they have not seen." In short, the church must be a place where "Kingdom qualities" are in evidence. There can be no place in the church for rivalry, racism, segregation, sexism, or greed. Righteousness must be our garment, justice our goal, love the means to all such ends.

Second, the church must be prepared to ask itself some hard questions if it wishes to be a city set on a hill—that is, if it wants to be an example for the world of God's reign and of the moral and spiritual qualities God requires of God's people.

Churches may well consider questions such as these: Why is eleven o'clock worship on Sunday mornings still the most segregated hour of the week for many congregations? Why do churches so often see benevolence ministries and offerings for the poor as burdens rather than as opportunities to be blessed? Why do many churches in North America spend up to ninety percent of their annual budgets on their own buildings, their own pastors, and on programs that chiefly benefit themselves, rather than on deeds of mercy or on sharing the gospel with those outside the walls of the church?

The early church was a missionary movement that also nurtured those already among the saints. In contrast, the modern church is a nurture institution that may also have a mission committee or mission budget. The question is, Which kind of church—the early church or the modern church—better manifests God's will and dominion?

When Jesus told stories about who would sit down at the messianic banquet when the dominion of God fully comes on earth, he reminded his followers that there would be some surprising people present: "I tell you, many will come from east and west and will eat with Abraham and Isaac and Jacob in the kingdom [dominion] of heaven, while the heirs of the kingdom [dominion] will be thrown into the outer darkness" (Matthew 8:11-12).

The question that such a strong warning raises is whether the church is a winsome place. In other words, is the church a place that the least, the last, and the lost find inviting and helpful? Is it a place where the least, the last, and the lost become the most, the first, and the found? Is the church—any church—a hospital for sick sinners or a museum for satisfied saints? Doing a better job of ministering to its community is one way the church can better manifest God's dominion.

Third, churches can be places of God's presence by having the kind of life-transforming worship and faith-forming teaching and fellowship that people are eager to come back to week after week. Such powerful worship and potent teaching and fellowship help people draw closer to God. Indeed, with the psalmist they exclaim: "I was glad when they said to me, 'Let us go to the house of the LORD!'" (Psalm 122:1). As the psalmists say repeatedly and in various ways, God dwells in the midst of the people's praises. Vital worship, teaching, and fellowship are clear manifestations of God's saving presence.

The early church had many faults, but the one fault it did not appear to have suffered from was being boring. Just look at the description of its worship found in 1 Corinthians 11–14: Worship involved singing, prophesying, preaching, speaking in tongues, praying, sharing in the Lord's Supper, eating a fellowship meal, listening to teaching and evaluating it, sharing words of encouragement, sharing news from the mission field, opening one's house for fellowship meetings, and a host of other things. There is only one report in the New Testament of a person going to sleep during worship; this was because the preacher went on late into the night, not because the service was dull! Early-church worship was a event that took several hours to complete—and few were eager to leave when it was over.

A fourth way that churches can manifest God's dominion is by having a solid, ongoing commitment to witness in their own communities and by supporting the work of missions throughout the world. It is worth remembering that at one point when Jesus was asked to speak about the future, he said that before God's will can fully be done on earth, before Christ can return, "the good news must first be proclaimed to all nations" (Mark 13:10). Similarly, Matthew concludes his Gospel with the Great Commission to make disciples of all nations (Matthew 28:19-20).

It is an open question as to how seriously the church takes these remarks. There are still hundreds of ethnic groups who do not have the Word of God available in their languages; yet Wycliffe Bible Translators and other valid ministries are always short on support from the church for translating and sharing the Scriptures. What would the church look like if it really took seriously the Great Commission? It certainly would look a lot more like a place where the dominion of God is coming on earth.

Last, churches can display God's dominion by being a family of love, grace, and caring. At one point during his ministry, Jesus remarked that the primary family for his followers should be the family of faith, not the biological family. Indeed, he said that whoever did God's will, and thus manifested God's dominion, was his brother, sister, or mother (Mark 3:31-35). A church that displays the Dominion is a church that not merely nurtures nuclear families but is a family to *all* its members.

We live in a world full of broken relationships; many people are single for a variety of reasons. These people are looking for love, support, and help—and, in some cases, healing. If the church is truly a family, then all people, not just married people, will find the church a place where God's saving and redeeming activity is evident. God's dominion is manifested in those fellowships where every person is affirmed as being of sacred worth, whether single or married, young or old, healthy or infirm, born or about to be born.

The Church as Servant of the Dominion

Finally, we need to say something about the difference between a church that manifests the dominion of God and a church that has a "domination mentality." A domination mentality shows itself when the church announces arrogantly that it is the sole dispenser of God's grace, and that the authority and decisions of its leaders should not be questioned. By contrast, a church that manifests the dominion of God recognizes that only God is God, and that the church's leaders are *servants* of God, not saviors.

A church that manifests the dominion of God recognizes that true leaders are servant-leaders; therefore, such a church does not indulge or encourage the "cult of personality" we sometimes find in churches where the loyalty of the people is centered around a powerful person instead of around Christ. A pastor who recognizes God's rule and saving work in the midst of his or her people will not think that he or she is indispensable to the church. Rather, as a servant of God, he or she will seek to *enable* the gifts and graces of the baptized, not *disable* them by trying to do or control all the church's ministries.

Jesus had very specific advice to his disciples about how they should lead so that their leadership makes clear that only God rules and saves. Jesus put it this way:

> The kings of the Gentiles lord it over them; and those in authority over them are called benefactors. But not so with you; rather the greatest among you must become like the youngest, and the leader like one who serves. For who is greater, the one who is at table or the one who serves? Is it not the one at the table? But I am among you as one who serves.
>
> (Luke 22:25-27)

Interestingly enough, those leaders—both clergy and lay—who model themselves after Christ's leadership style do not assume the *position* of the church's Lord but rather the *posture* of the Lord, namely, that of a servant. It is precisely this posture of a servant that helps to prevent the development of a domination mentality, either in the pastor or in the parishioners.

Conclusion

In this chapter, we discussed the location—the place—of God's dominion on earth. We stressed that while the Dominion cannot be *confined* to the context of God's gathered people, the church may nevertheless be considered the preeminent place of God's reign on earth. God's dominion refers to God's saving activity among human beings; and in the church this redemptive activity manifests itself in corporate worship and in a variety of works of charity and piety, including sharing the gospel and working for justice in human relationships and in society. In the next chapter, we ask a more personal question: How does the Dominion manifest itself in the individual believer's life?

Questions for Reflection

1 Where is God's dominion preeminently found on earth?

2 Why can the church not simply be equated with God's dominion?

3 What are the qualities that indicate that a church is manifesting the presence of the Dominion?

4 List several aspects of the church's worship, fellowship, and service that make evident God's saving presence in its life.

5 What is the difference between a church that displays a domination mentality and a church that manifests the dominion of God?

6 In a church that manifests God's dominion, what is the model for church leaders?

CHAPTER THREE

Taking the Dominion Personally

I t is easy enough to talk about God's reign in the abstract, or even about how it manifests itself in the church or in the world. But how do we discern whether the dominion of God—the lordship of Christ—is present in an individual's life? Are there concrete ways—"evidence," if you will—that show the transforming power of God's presence in the Christian's words and deeds?

As we will see in this chapter, the chief evidence of the Dominion in the believer's life is *holiness of heart and life*. Furthermore, there are several "spiritual inventories" or "litmus tests" in the New Testament that list a variety of concrete behaviors and attitudes that the person who belongs to God's dominion should strive to emulate. Exhibiting these behaviors and attitudes is essential to cultivating a life of holiness.

The Entrance Requirements of the Dominion

At one point during his ministry, Jesus said that unless a person receives the Dominion like a child, he or she will never enter the dominion of God in the future (Mark 10:15). Jesus also remarked that children should be allowed to come to him because "it is to such as these that the kingdom [dominion] of God belongs" (Mark 10:14).

Jesus' comments are remarkable in several regards. First, Jesus is responding to the disciples who were speaking sternly to people bringing their children to Jesus for his blessing. The disciples seem to have assumed that Jesus' teaching and an encounter with Jesus was for adults only. This kind of assumption was not uncommon in antiquity. In early Judaism, for example, children were never sent off to study with famous rabbis or Jewish teachers (such as Jesus). The Lord, however, insists that there is a place in God's dominion for children; in fact, even adults cannot enter the Dominion unless they take on certain childlike qualities. Requiring that adults enter God's dominion like a child is truly astonishing since in antiquity the child was never set up as a model of discipleship—at least not until Jesus came along.

What, then, does it mean to say that one cannot enter the dominion of God unless one receives it like a child? To begin with, I suspect that Jesus had in mind the fact that children have no difficulty receiving gifts. Indeed, most everything children receive comes as a gift, not as something they have earned. Have you ever noticed how at Christmastime children have no difficulty receiving gifts without immediately wondering who they must repay? Many adults, on the other hand, find it hard accepting a gift from someone for whom they have not bought a gift in return because it makes them uncomfortable.

Why is this? I suspect it is in part because our society tells us repeatedly, "You don't get something for nothing" or, "You get what you pay for or earn." Our society is fundamentally *works-*

oriented and not *grace-centered.* That is, we like to think of ourselves as people who don't need any help. Given an opportunity,
we can get for ourselves whatever we need. In short, we like to
be independent.

A child, on the other hand, knows very well that he or she is
dependent on others. Children don't delude themselves into
thinking that to truly own something one must have earned it or
must have received it through some kind of "you-scratch-my-
back-I'll-scratch-yours" routine. *A child knows how to receive;* and
this includes knowing how to receive the Dominion, the saving
rule of God in one's life.

One of my best friends grew up with a friend named Sandy,
who was a talented and sensitive young man. But Sandy's heart
was not open to the Lord, in part because of what had happened
to his sister. Sandy's sister became very ill when still quite young
and was taken to the hospital, where she received a rather grim
prognosis. Yet this girl of five or six years of age had a strong
faith in Jesus, and whenever Sandy came to see her, she would
ask him, "Have you met my Jesus? Have you seen him?"

The relentless testimony of his little sister was eventually to
change Sandy's life, but not until after she died in the hospital.
Today Sandy is a priest, serving God in a monastery. His life
truly bears witness to the meaning of the words "and a little
child shall lead them" (Isaiah 11:6). It was a child who showed
Sandy how to receive God's dominion—namely, with absolute
trust in Jesus and an openness to receiving the saving rule of
God in one's life. Such radical trust and unconditional openness
are an essential part of what Jesus had in mind when he said
that we must receive God's dominion like a child.

It's difficult to pinpoint why we often seem reticent to surrender totally to God's will and rule for our lives. Sometimes it
seems to be because we don't totally trust what God will do
with us. And, as we all know, it is difficult—if not impossible—
to fully love someone whom one doesn't trust completely. This

is as true of human relationships, such as the marriage bond, as it is of one's relationship with God. Those of us who find it difficult to totally surrender to the lordship of Christ can always pray for more faith and grace in our lives. On the other hand, we can take courage from the example of those who exhibit a childlike faith and accept the reign of God in their lives unconditionally—like Sandy's sister.

Are we prepared to receive the Dominion like a child, allowing God to be Lord of our lives? Are we ready for God—not us—to set the agenda for what we say and do, for how we behave, for the career we choose, for the path we take in life? Above all, are we prepared to give God our unconditional loyalty and to place our trust unconditionally in God?

The fact that, according to Mark, the Dominion is made up of children and those who are like children suggests that we obtain a place in the Dominion by God's grace, not by our own strenuous effort to secure it. If we think we can work or worm our way into God's good graces, we are sadly mistaken. The dominion of God must be received with childlike faith and trust; it cannot be earned or bargained for, much less bought.

Have we allowed the "you-scratch-my-back-I'll-scratch-yours" mentality of our culture to shape our vision of how to relate to the dominion of God? Are we really prepared to grasp and accept the concept of *grace*—that is, God's unmerited favor, the undeserved benefits God bestows simply because *that is what God is like?* God's grace-filled rule in our lives is consistent with God's loving character. That character is revealed in the fact that God so loved us that God cared enough to send the very best— God's only Son—to save us (John 3:16). And the Son, Jesus, perfectly revealed God's unconditional love—God's unmerited grace—in what he said and did while he was among us.

The Character of the Dominion

While the Dominion is foremost about what God's character is like, it is also clear about what the lives of those who live under God's reign should look like. The New Testament contains a number of "character descriptions" of the Christian as bearer of the Dominion. Some of these descriptions are found in passages such as Galatians 5:16-26; 1 Corinthians 13; and Matthew 5–7. We will take a look at these texts in the pages to follow.

Sometimes we may be forgiven for thinking that the clearest evidence that we are living under God's reign is that we have a variety of flashy spiritual gifts to use for glorifying God and edifying others. While it is true that the presence of spiritual gifts in a person's life is evidence of God's work and rule, the gifts of the Spirit must be normed by the fruit of the Spirit. That means that *Christian character*, rather than talent or giftedness, is a clearer sign of the reign of God in a person's life.

What do texts such as Galatians 5:16-26; 1 Corinthians 13; and Matthew 5–7 tell us about Christian character? Let's take a look. All three passages make clear that *love* is at the heart of the matter. The clearest sign of God's rule in a person's life is that he or she is a loving human being, prepared to manifest the sort of self-sacrificial giving that Jesus showed when he was on earth. One of the ways I check my own progress in grace—or "sanctification," as this journey is sometimes—is to ask myself every once in a while, *Am I a more loving person today than I was this time a month ago, or a year ago?* If God is working in our lives, and if God's rule is extending to more and more areas of our lives, then we should be able to see progress in manifesting Christlike qualities.

Galatians 5:16-26

Whenever I examine Galatians 5:16-26 I am struck not just by the list of the fruit of the Spirit but also by the list of things with which that fruit is contrasted: sexual immorality, idolatry, enmities, strife, jealousy, anger, quarrels, factions, drunkenness, among others (verses 19-21). Notice that these are all forms of human behavior that divide people, that break up homes, that destroy relationships; in short, they are all forms of self-centered and self-seeking behavior.

Let's take a closer look at the list of the fruit of the Spirit found in Galatians 5. The passage identifies the following fruit: "love, joy, peace, patience, kindness, generosity, faithfulness, gentleness, and self-control" (verses 22-23). Notice that because the Spirit's fruit is *God-centered* and *other-directed*, it consists of qualities that bring and bind people together; that make for lasting relationships with friends, spouses, and families; and that foster an enduring relationship with God in Christ. Notice also that Paul is not speaking of the *fruits* (plural) of the Spirit but of the *fruit* (singular). The singular *fruit* implies that *all* the Spirit's fruit (mentioned in verses 22-23) should be manifested in the life of each Christian. We don't choose the fruit of the Spirit we want to display.

Also, the fruit referred to in these verses is something *God* produces in our lives by the Spirit; these are not character traits we have had since birth. When the Holy Spirit rules in our lives, we should expect to see all—not just one or two—of these Spirit-bestowed traits manifested. And if we don't see evidence of all the fruit of the Spirit in our lives, we know which areas of our lives to pray about, asking God to help us grow in grace so that the Dominion may advance in our lives.

I am impressed by how much the character description in Galatians 5 depicts the character of Christ himself. Christ is the one who brought love, joy, and peace. He is the one who was kind to the lost, generous to the poor and to the poor in Spirit, faithful to his word and to his disciples, and gentle in laying his yoke of discipleship on others. Above all, Christ was always in control of his life, even to the point that when he was tempted to do something that was not God's will, he would remember to pray: "Yet, not my will but yours be done" (Luke 22:42).

1 Corinthians 13

Paul's portrayal of love in 1 Corinthians 13 has also often been said to be an apt description of the character of Christ, just as it is intended to be a benchmark by which Christians measure progress in conforming to the image of Christ. Consider verses 4-8:

> Love is patient; love is kind; love is not envious or boastful or arrogant or rude. It does not insist on its own way; it is not irritable or resentful; it does not rejoice in wrongdoing, but rejoices in the truth. It bears all things, believes all things, hopes all things, endures all things. Love never ends.

Just as Jesus' life of love perfectly manifested God's rule, so loving as Jesus did should be the goal of our lives as Christians. When others look at what we say and do, they ought to see Jesus; and in seeing Jesus, they ought to see a glimpse of the dominion of God.

Sometimes Christianity is mistakenly assumed to be a religion that inculcates weakness rather than strength in people, that eviscerates human personality rather than strengthening it. The meek are the weak, the humble are the inferior—so the argument goes. Yet the Christian's model for meekness and humility is Jesus himself. If there was one person who walked this earth who was not weak—not even in the face of supernatural evil—it was Jesus. He didn't back down from the power of evil, even when it came in the form of a cross. Furthermore, if there was one person on this earth who did not suffer from an inferiority complex, it was Jesus. If there was ever one person who was sure of who he was and what he ought to do with his life, it was Jesus.

It follows from this that if Christ is the example of humility, then humility has nothing to do with feelings of low self-worth or with deeds that degrade the self. Rather, as Philippians 2:4-11 makes clear, humility has to do with a choice we make: I deliberately choose to make sacrifices; I deliberately put the interests of others ahead of my own so that they may prosper. I choose to be a servant of others, not their lord—whether it be in my church or in my business, with my family or with my friends.

The choice to be humble takes character *strength,* not character *weakness.* Just as it takes a person of strong character to walk away and not to fight back when someone strikes him or her, so it takes a person of strong—not weak—character to willingly make sacrifices for others. Most important, the choice to be humble displays the character of Christ—the character of love. It makes evident the presence of the dominion of God in a human life.

Matthew 5–7

Matthew 5-7 is often considered the blueprint for Christian discipleship. It is also a good litmus test to tell whether the dominion of God is working its will in our lives. It should be said from the outset that it is quite impossible to follow this blueprint if we are talking about merely human effort. What Jesus asks of us here is possible only if God's grace is at work in our lives.

Consider what Jesus is asking of us in these chapters from Matthew: Do not insult or berate others. If you have anything against someone else—or if you discover that someone else is upset with *you*—then before you worship in church or give offerings to God, go and be reconciled with that brother or sister. Otherwise, how can we pray: "Forgive us our debts, as we also have forgiven our debtors" (Matthew 6:12)?

A story I once heard illustrates this well. On Communion Sunday shortly after the Civil War, in a Presbyterian church in Richmond, Virginia, an extraordinary thing happened. For many years it had been the custom for the white families and their slaves all to partake of Communion, but separately, with the slaves being served last. On this particular Sunday, when the pastor announced the call for people to come forward and take

Communion, an elderly black man (a former slave) stood up with the white worshipers and began walking to the Communion rail. The white people all froze in disbelief, except one elderly, graybearded, white gentleman in the back of the church. He came forward, took the black man by the arm, walked with him to the Communion rail, and together they partook of the Lord's Supper. That white gentleman was Robert E. Lee, the famous Confederate general. After that experience, there was no more separate Communion in that church. Being reconciled to others is costly and difficult, but that is what Jesus asks of anyone who professes to belong to the Dominion.

But there's more. Jesus asks of us not merely to refrain from *acts* of sexual infidelity and immorality; he asks us to quench any such *thoughts* we may have (Matthew 5:27-28). Not only are we not to swear falsely, but we are not to swear *at all*. Our word should be our bond; our yes should mean yes and our no mean no (Matthew 5:33-37). Jesus asks of us not to resist an evildoer. If we are struck an insulting blow, we are to turn the other cheek and accept the other person rather than retaliate (Matthew 5:38-39). Jesus calls us to live nonviolent lives, to be proactive rather than reactive when bad things happen to us. Furthermore, if someone takes from us something he or she truly needs, such as clothing, Jesus asks that we be prepared to give that person even more: "Give to everyone who begs from you, and do not refuse anyone who wants to borrow from you" (Matthew 5:42).

By asking us to give freely of our belongings to anyone in need, Jesus calls us to love more than just our friends and family; indeed, he asks us to love even our enemies, those who wish to do us harm. Love of enemies is said to be a godlike quality; it surely goes against every natural *human* instinct. Therefore, wherever we see someone loving his or her enemy, there we see evidence of the grace of God at work. Such love happens only because of the supernatural rule of God; it happens only where the Dominion is present.

Corrie ten Boom was once confronted by the need to forgive a particularly heinous enemy. She and her sister Betsie were placed in a Nazi prison camp during World War II. During that time, Betsie died before her eyes, emaciated. Even when she was on her deathbed, Betsie insisted that she and Corrie bring the healing love of Jesus to the German people.

Years later, after Corrie had been miraculously released from the death camp and was sharing the gospel in defeated Germany, a man came up to her, stuck out his hand, and said, "You mentioned Ravensbruck in your talk. I was a guard there.... But since that time, I have become a Christian. I know that God has forgiven me for the cruel things I did there, but I would like to hear it from your lips as well.... Will you forgive me?"

At first Corrie was reluctant to forgive the guard, remembering the unspeakably cruel deeds he had done. Then, remembering Jesus' injunction to forgive everyone—including our enemies—she slowly took the man's hand and said, "I forgive you, brother!... With all my heart." Forgiving her enemy was not a natural response for Corrie ten Boom, but it was the sort of action that showed the presence of God's reign in her life.[1]

Jesus goes on in Matthew 6 to ask us to give charitably, to pray meaningfully, to fast regularly, and to save sparingly. He also asks of us not to serve two masters: God and money. Jesus knows that when money has dominion over a person's heart and mind, it is a harsh taskmaster. Since money and possessions can never fill up the God-shaped vacuum in the human heart, we never feel as if we have enough; we are always dissatisfied. It is easy to see why Jesus compares money to serving a god. For when we place our total trust in our assets, they become our god; they rule our lives. Preoccupation with our assets dictates how we act, when we spend our money, to whom we give, whom we associate with, and so forth. When money becomes our god, our motive for acting is always enlightened self-interest

---

1 Adapted and reprinted by permission from *Guideposts Magazine*. Copyright © 1972 by Guideposts, Carmel, NY 10512.

instead of the prompting of God's love for the world. Not sur-prisingly, immediately after speaking about money, Jesus speaks about worry (Matthew 6:25-34).

In my own experience, some of the least happy people I have ever met have been the wealthy. These people always worry about protecting what they own, their investments, and the like. Rather than living by faith in God, they live out of fear of what might happen to them and to what they have accumulated. The parable in Luke 12:13-21 of the rich man who stored away an abundance of possessions in his barns but then died before he was able to enjoy the benefits of all his hard work, stands as a reminder of Jesus' point about money and possessions: Life is short; therefore, we should love much and live on the basis of trust in God and not in our own resources. Only God can pro-vide a security that is eternal. It is a sign of the presence of God's reign in our lives when we are generous and prepared to make financial sacrifices to further the cause of the Dominion.

Toward the end of the Sermon on the Mount, Jesus speaks about the subject of self-deception regarding one's relationship with God (Matthew 7:21-23). The essence of Jesus' words is this: We may give lip service to the Lord, or even speak powerful words or do mighty deeds in Jesus' name, but if we don't do the will of God, we won't enter God's dominion. In this passage Jesus appears to have in mind not primarily the nominal believer but rather those people who exercise the gifts of God for their own glory or aggrandizement. Again Jesus' warning is salutary: Godly character, and not goodly gifts and talents in themselves, is the indicator of God's rule in a person's life.

The final exhortation of the Sermon on the Mount—to be doers of God's Word and not merely hearers—reminds us, how-ever, that Jesus expects us to work out in daily living what God is working in us (Matthew 7:24-29). We need to *act* on the basis of the inward renovations God is making in our lives. Words without deeds are empty; but, equally, deeds done for the wrong reasons and to the wrong ends will not manifest the presence of God's dominion in our lives.

The Dominion and the Call to Holiness

The discussion thus far about the character descriptions of those who belong to the Dominion has prepared us to examine more closely the issue of *holiness*, or *sanctification*. Some people think of holiness as one (perhaps impossible!) trait of Christian character among others. Actually, holiness is another, more comprehensive, way of speaking about the purpose of salvation. For holiness means striving to manifest the character of God on earth through our worship and our service—indeed, through *every aspect of our daily lives*. As God is holy love, so we also are to be holy and loving.

Now, holiness does not mean having a holier-than-thou attitude. This is a constant danger for believing people. That is why Jesus warns that we should not judge other people, lest we be judged in the same fashion (Matthew 7:1). When Jesus says, "Do not judge," he does not mean that we should not be discerning about how we evaluate human behavior; we certainly should be. Rather, the issue is that *we* are not the ones deciding another person's eternal destiny; nor are we able to discern the intent of their hearts. Therefore, we must leave the fate of other people in God's hands and attend to the spiritual health of our own lives. However, we *do* have the moral responsibility to lovingly warn a brother or sister when we sense that he or she is going astray and is thus imperiling his or her spiritual life and potentially his or her place in God's final dominion.

What, then, does holiness of heart and life mean? It means at least two things: (1) hallowing all of life (great and small), seeing all of it as the gift of a gracious God and therefore of sacred worth; and (2) purity of heart and behavior. The commitment to ethical integrity is crucial, for we are called upon to manifest the character of Christ to the world.

Recently we have seen a variety of jewelry with the letters *W.W.J.D.* on them. These letters remind us that before we act, we should always ask: What would Jesus do? This is a very good question. The story is told of a medical missionary who ministered in Armenia during the nineteenth century. On one occasion, a small man who was near death and enduring much suffering was brought to him for medical care. The doctor slowly ministered the man back to health, but he also shared the gospel of Christ with his patient. In due course the man became both physically well and a Christian. He returned to his village and, like many a new convert, he could hardly stop talking about Jesus. At one point an irritated listener asked, "Why should I believe you? You have never even seen this Jesus. On your own account of things, he died over fifteen-hundred years ago." Undaunted, the little man responded immediately, "To the contrary, I have seen the doctor, and Christ lives in him. Further-more, Christ now lives in me."

Holiness means manifesting in one's life the lifestyle of Christ himself, his purity and power, his graciousness and humility. Although holiness does mean that we refrain from doing sins and misdeeds—Galatians 5:16-21 makes that clear—it is not primarily about who we are *not* or what we *don't* do; rather, holiness is primarily about who we *are* and what we are to *do*. Holiness, then, is primarily about what we are called to manifest in our lives—namely, the reign of God.

Awareness of God's reign in one's life necessarily changes one's view of life and of the world, and of what is important about living in this world. For one thing, a person who lives under the reign of God does not view this life as the be-all and end-all of existence. She or he does not go around saying things such as, "You go around only once in life, so grab for all the gusto you can get." No, a Christian is one who lives in the light of *eternity*, manifesting the perspective of eternity *here on earth*. Therefore, the believer does not have to clutch onto this earthly existence as if it is all there is to life. And precisely for this reason, a person who has eternal life feels the freedom to give her or his life for the sake of God's dominion, should that ever become necessary.

Not only does a Christian with a "Kingdom perspective" not feel the need to cling to physical life, but he or she also has no desire to clutch onto material resources. Instead, such a Christian trusts God and gives generously. The same attitude applies to *what* and *whom* the believer loves. The person under God's reign has been freed to love graciously, to love all people, to love indiscriminately. One of my fellow New Testament scholars likes to say that Christian love is not like a heat-seeking missile, prompted by something inherently attractive in the target. Rather, Christian love gives to all and sundry because it is the right thing—the Christlike thing—to do.

Holiness as Counter-Cultural Discipleship

At this point you may wonder if living the life of holiness requires a counter-cultural lifestyle. The answer depends on how Christian the dominant culture is in which one lives. In an increasingly secular culture such as the United States of America, a counter-cultural approach is becoming increasingly necessary because the dominant culture no longer endorses Christian values.

Counter-cultural Christianity can take many forms. It may involve an economic boycott against companies that peddle pornography, which degrades both women and the men who buy it. It may mean protesting a war because the gospel requires that we love our enemies. It may involve working constructively against the marginalization of society's weakest members: the elderly, the infirm, the unborn, the poor.

A counter-cultural lifestyle may take the form of assisting people who have experienced calamity, without waiting for the government to take care of them. While living in northeast Ohio,

I was struck by how the Amish community began rebuilding their houses and barns immediately after a tornado devastated the region. Most of the other inhabitants, including non-Amish Christians, stood around wringing their hands, angry about the slow response of the government to the disaster. Counter-cultural Christianity doesn't wait for a secular government to show compassion; it knows it must act on its own.

If a counter-cultural lifestyle of holiness is becoming increasingly necessary for the church under God's rule, it means that God's people must recover (or do a better job with) many of the responsibilities that the church considered part of its mission in ages past: caring for the elderly and the marginalized, building homes, and working for the transformation of societal values. These responsibilities, too, are part of what it means to manifest God's reign upon the earth—to live a holy life. Personal sanctification is necessary, but Christians are not called to live in isolation. Rather, God places them in communities of faith; therefore, believers must take seriously the *social* dimension of holiness. Christ's character must be manifested not just by individual Christians but also by the body of Christ. Only in this way will the dominion of God truly come on this earth.

Conclusion

In the first three chapters of this book, we concentrated on the *present* dimension of God's dominion on earth. Yet it would be myopic to stop the discussion of the Dominion at this point, for there are at least as many passages in the New Testament that focus on the *future* manifestation of God's dominion on earth as there are passages that speak of the Dominion in the present.

What will it be like when God's future dominion breaks fully into human history? How may we prepare for its coming? These are some of the issues we will address in the second half of this study.

Questions for Reflection

1 What did Jesus mean when he said that we must receive God's reign like a child?

2 What attributes of a child, do you think, did Jesus want his disciples to emulate?

3 What are the fruits of the Spirit, and how do they affect human relationships?

4 What does the term *holiness* mean? How is holiness different from being "holier-than-thou"?

5 What is the connection between a holy lifestyle and a counter-cultural lifestyle?

Part Two

The
Glorious
Future

CHAPTER FOUR

"Thy Kingdom Come"

Many people have no problem coming up with potent *images* of what the Dominion will look like when it comes fully on earth: "The wolf shall live with the lamb" (Isaiah 11:6); "They shall beat their swords into plowshares" (Isaiah 2:4). Yet many of these people find it hard to *believe* in this future dimension of God's dominion. Even some Christians would argue that after two thousand years, Jesus is probably not coming back to bring human history to a climax.

On the other hand, thousands of other people today have lost any viable hope for the future of *this* world and have replaced that hope with an other-worldly hope—the hope of going to heaven when they die. Such an attitude is surely understandable in light of the suffering, the terror, and the hopelessness facing so many people every day. Yet this failure of nerve and of faith is not justifiable; indeed, it is often grounded in a misunderstanding of what the New Testament actually says about the future of God's dominion.

The Expectation of the Dominion

G iving up hope for this world and frantically anticipating another world on the part of some people raises the question: When exactly will God bring the Dominion to completion? To answer this question, we need to note three things: First, the New Testament says nothing explicit about the *timing* of the second coming of Christ; it simply affirms the *fact* of that coming. Indeed, according to Mark 13:32, Jesus said that even *he* didn't know when the Son of Man will come. Second, often when discussing the time of Christ's coming again, we fail to bear in mind that God is not a creature bound by the space-time universe. God transcends time and is not limited by time as we know it within the material universe. This is part of the meaning of 2 Peter 3:8-10:

> But...with the Lord one day is like a thousand years, and a thousand years are like one day. The Lord is not slow about his promise,...but is patient with you, not wanting any to perish, but all to come to repentance. But the day of the Lord will come like a thief.

Third, the earliest Christians, since they did not know when Christ would return, were prepared to reckon with and hope for the possibility that Christ would return in their own day. However, they used images such as "a thief in the night" to convey the fact that Christ would come at a surprising or unexpected time; therefore, they should always be ready.

While the New Testament authors believed robustly *that* the Lord would return, they did not try to stipulate the exact *timing* of his return. It is a mistake, therefore, to suggest that the earliest Christians believed that Christ would definitely return during their own lifetime, and that when that proved untrue, they had to conjure with the delay of the Royal Return. The viable future of God's dominion on earth should not be dismissed on the basis of a misreading of what the New Testament claims about the timing of Christ's return.

The Dominion and the Future of Heaven and Earth

It is not just the Second Coming and its timing that creates controversy. Many people raise questions about what the term *heaven* means, and the relation of heaven to the coming of God's dominion on earth. Let's take a look at some of these issues.

The Lord's Prayer, which the church should pray in good faith, includes the words "thy kingdom come, thy will be done, on earth as it is in heaven." This prayer makes clear that God's dominion in heaven is not the same as God's future dominion on earth; otherwise, there would be no point to this petition. The petition suggests that the Dominion is already fully present in heaven, but not yet so on earth.

With this in mind, let us consider the meaning of the term *heaven*. By definition, *heaven* is "the dwelling place of God." Some scholars have deduced from this that because God is omnipresent (present everywhere) in the material universe, heaven is likewise present everywhere in our world. This view misunderstands the concept of God's omnipresence. The Bible does not suggest that a little bit of God is everywhere, in all things in the material universe. This notion has rightly been dubbed *pantheism* (from the Greek *pan* that means "all," and *theos* that means "God"). The God of the Bible is not a substance or a force that permeates all things. God is a personal being; indeed, God is a tri-personal being: Father, Son, and Holy Spirit. When the Bible says that God is present everywhere, it is saying that all things are present to God *at once*; for God is much greater than the material universe. God is not an item *within* the universe but the Maker *of* it.

When we speak of "heaven," then, we must remember that we are not referring to a place within the material universe, say, just outside the earth's atmosphere. Instead, we are speaking of the eternal dwelling place of God, from where God created the *whole* universe.

Furthermore, God should be distinguished from heaven itself. For instance, God can be near, in our midst, while heaven still can be remote. This means that while God is dwelling within God's people through the Holy Spirit, heaven does *not* now exist on earth. However, the future of God's dominion does involve, as it were, a merger of heaven and earth. That is, God will make God's final and eternal dwelling place with those who dwell below. At that point, heaven will come down and earth will be transformed.

Another indication that heaven does not now exist on earth is found in the fact that the New Testament speaks of believers as dying and going *to* heaven. (See, for example, the parable of the rich man and Lazarus in Luke 16:19-31.) However, a point that many modern readers miss is that the New Testament does not envision heaven as the *final* dwelling place of God's people. Notice that when Scripture speaks of the final future of God's people, it talks about the resurrection of the dead. This suggests that the final destination of God's people has to do with life in a new *embodied* condition *on earth*, not a disembodied existence in heaven. In other words, the ultimate future of humankind has nothing to do with a ghostly existence somewhere outside the material universe; rather, it involves living in a resurrection-body in space and time.

Resurrection and the Fullness of the Dominion

Let's take a closer look at the meaning of the phrase "the resurrection of the dead." In particular, let us explore the connection between this phrase and the resurrection of Christ.

The Apostles' Creed, which the church has affirmed for centuries, includes the words:

> I believe in Jesus Christ…
>> On the third day he rose again;
>> he ascended into heaven,
>> is seated at the right hand of the Father,
>> and will come again to judge the living and the dead.
> I believe in…
>> the resurrection of the body
>> and the life everlasting.[2]

Note first that the resurrection of the body—that is, the resurrection of the dead—is not a novel doctrine; the church has always affirmed it. Note further that the second reference to resurrection—"I believe in…the resurrection of the body"—refers not to the resurrection of *Jesus* but to the resurrection of *believers*.

Moreover, according to the Creed, the resurrection of the dead is contingent upon the return of Christ. The former will not transpire unless or until the latter happens. Indeed, one can say that the whole schedule of eschatological (end-time) events hinges on the return of Christ. Until and unless Christ returns, there will be no resurrection of the dead, no final judgment, no life everlasting, no dominion of God on earth.

In many ways, the return of Christ "triggers" the resurrection of the dead. As Paul puts it in 1 Corinthians 15:14: If Christ has not been raised, then the dead will not be raised either. Indeed, if Christ has not been raised, then our faith is in vain, and we are still in our sins. As with so many things in the Christian faith, a proper understanding of the career of Christ—both his past and future career—leads to a proper understanding of our future and the future of God's dominion. That is to say, God's dominion began during Jesus' ministry, reached its first climactic point with the resurrection of Jesus, and will be completed when Christ comes again.

---

2 From *The United Methodist Hymnal* (Nashville: The United Methodist Publishing House, 1989), 882.

Christ and the Future of the Dominion

Let us define a bit more carefully the connection between Christ's life, death, and resurrection, and the ultimate future of God's dominion. To do this, let us consider more fully 1 Corinthians 15. This is one of the most important passages in the New Testament dealing with the future of believers and the dominion of God.

More than likely, we are all familiar with key verses from 1 Corinthians 15 (for example, verses 3-5); we often recite them at Easter. But it is also in this same chapter that Paul provides a brief sketch of the future. According to the Apostle, Christ is raised as the "first fruits" of the resurrection from the dead; then at his coming, those who belong to Christ are raised (1 Corinthians 15:23).

> [Afterward] comes the end, when he hands over the kingdom [dominion] to God the Father, after he has destroyed every ruler and every authority and power. For he must reign until he has put all his enemies under his feet. The last enemy to be destroyed is death.... When all things are subjected to him, then the Son himself will also be subjected to the one who put all things in subjection under him, so that God may be all in all.
>
> (1 Corinthians 15:24-26, 28)

For Paul, the resurrection of believers is no different from the resurrection of the Lord himself: The risen Christ is the "first fruits"; those who are in Christ are the "latter fruits." The Apostle makes clear that the believer's *future* will be like Christ's *past*. This implies several things.

First, Christ has already been raised from the dead, while for believers resurrection is still an event in the future. Second, as the example of Christ shows, existence is always *embodied* existence—first in a physical body and then in a resurrection body. It will be no different for those who are in Christ (1 Corinthians 15:42-49). Third, unlike the physical body, the resurrection body is immune to disease, decay, and death, for it is imperishable (verses 53-54). Incidentally, although resurrection is something that happens to dead people, Paul does affirm that there will be believers alive on earth when Christ returns; however, they too will be transformed into a resurrection state (verse 51).

Notice that in speaking in Chapter 15 of the final future for believers, Paul refers twice to the dominion of God. He stresses the fact that in their current mortal state, believers cannot participate in the *final form* of God's dominion. To participate in that imperishable new creation, one must also be in an imperishable condition; specifically, one must have a resurrection body like Christ's. Furthermore, when Christ has accomplished all that God had sent him to do at and after the Second Coming—namely, set up the final form of God's rule on earth—he will return the Dominion to the Father, who will reign over all things forever.

Two conclusions about the Dominion follow from this: First, the *final form* of God's reign on earth is not yet a reality: 1 Corinthians 15:24 and 15:28 link closely both future salvation and future judgment to what Christ will *yet* do when he returns. Second, the final form of the Dominion will be a reality here *on earth.* That is, the goal of God is not merely to reign in or from heaven, but to reign upon the *earth* forever. In God's plan creation, like human creatures, has a future, not least because God cares about all that God has made.

The important point to be made about our discussion thus far is that if one can believe that God raised Christ from the dead two thousand years ago, one should, in principle, have no difficulty with the concept of the resurrection of believers in the future. The *timing* of the event is surely a secondary issue compared with the *possibility* of the event.

Heaven, Earth, and the Scope of the Dominion

The consummation of the dominion of God does not happen when believers die and go to heaven; rather, the Dominion will be complete only when God's full reign—even over death—

becomes a reality *on earth*. That means that when we pray, "Thy kingdom come, thy will be done…," we are praying for the return of Christ, the resurrection of the dead, the last judgment, and for the life that comes when the Dominion is finally fully manifested on earth.

It is, of course, true that God's dominion—God's perfect reign—is already happening in heaven; however, this should not lead us to *equate* heaven and the Dominion. Heaven is currently a place, and God's dominion is the condition of that place. However, the Dominion is also in part the condition of the life of believers on earth right now. Christians manifest in a variety of ways the reality of the Dominion on earth here and now. The Dominion—God's saving reign—thus involves both heaven and earth, and one day will *encompass* both heaven and earth.

From what we have said thus far, it should be clear that there has been, is, and will always be a historical dimension or expression to God's dominion. God is not content simply to reign in heaven. Indeed, the whole New Testament is about a God who loved the world so much that he sent his Son to establish the Dominion *on earth*, as in heaven.

The historical nature of God's dominion means that Christians can never afford to devalue either creation or its future— whether we are talking about those bits of creation known as our bodies, or the rest of creation (both animate and inanimate). It is just poor theology to say, "This world is not where I belong; I'm only traveling through," as if heaven were all that really mattered. Indeed, the New Testament suggests just the opposite: Heaven is *not* the believer's home; it is simply a place through which he or she passes between the time of death and the time when he or she is raised from the dead.

It is of course true, as Paul says, that "we would rather be away from the body and at home with the Lord" (2 Corinthians 5:8). Often life in heaven is preferable to the suffering and sorrow and the pain and dying we face while on earth (Philippians

1:20-25). But there are actually three states that need to be compared: life in the flesh here on earth, life in heaven, and life in the resurrection body in the world to come. Paul unequivocally states that he would prefer to live on this earth until the resurrection and then be "clothed" with a resurrection body, rather than to die (2 Corinthians 5:4-5). The state of ultimate bliss is life on earth in the resurrection body.

It is no accident that the historic ritual of the church for funerals speaks primarily of the hope of resurrection, rather than of the hope of life without a body in heaven. (See also "A Service of Death and Resurrection" in *The United Methodist Hymnal*, 870.) Resurrection is a death-defying event. Resurrection makes clear that God is Lord not only of life but also of death. Resurrection shows us that God's yes is louder than death's no. Resurrection makes evident that God's rule will be established on earth as it is in heaven. Resurrection makes God's dominion on earth a historical reality, not just a vain hope.

The Historical Nature of the Dominion

This is a good place to say a bit more about Christianity as a historical religion. Our faith as Christians is in part grounded in what God has already accomplished in the history of Israel and in the history of Jesus Christ. Christians don't have faith in "faith," nor is Christian faith wishful thinking about the future.

Instead, we believe that God has *already* raised Jesus from the dead. On the basis of that historical event, we believe that God can perform such a miracle again for those who love him. Christ's history—his own real-life story—is the basis for our hope that one day God's dominion will fully come on the earth.

Christianity, then, is not a religion based on a "philosophy of life." It is based on specific irreducible facts of history—in particular, the facts of the death and resurrection of Christ. The historical reality of Christ's death and resurrection is crucial for Christian faith; for if Christ was not raised from the dead, Christians would have no point in talking about the future of God's dominion on earth. If there has not been and will be no resurrection, then the petition "Thy kingdom come" could never be answered here below in any full sense. Without the reality of Christ's resurrection, Christians can at best resign themselves to an other-worldly hope for the future. They certainly would have no basis for expecting God's sovereign rule over the forces of darkness, disease, decay, and death here below.

The New Testament bears significant witness to the historical character and locale of God's dominion, precisely because God's intent is to rule in *this world*, not just in heaven. That is what God's interventions in human history—God's acts of salvation— are all about. To speak only of God's dominion in heaven is to give up on God's claim on the creation. In a lost world, the transformed lives of believers are the beachhead of God's dominion on earth; they are tangible signs of God's reign. But we must hasten to add that God is not content to reign only in the lives of believers. God is the God of *all* the earth. However, to make possible God's universal reign on earth requires further divine incursion in history; and chief among these is the second coming of Christ.

The Dominion and the Timing of the End

Fascination with the year 2000 and with end-time speculation is alive and well, if supermarket tabloids are anything to go by. By all accounts, as the year 2000 draws closer, end-time forecasting will increasingly heat up.

What are sensible Christians to make of all this hype and hysteria? They can begin by keeping several important points in mind: First, Jesus was born somewhere between 4 and 6 B.C.E. (Before the Common Era). That means the year 2000 has no particular import for biblical prophecy, since we passed the 2000-year mark from the time of Christ's birth several years ago! Second, as we said earlier, all previous predictions about the timing of the return of Christ have one thing in common: They have all been one-hundred percent wrong. Earnestness and fervor about the timing of the final events of human history do not equal knowledge about such things. Third, the New Testament speaks a lot about the end time, but it does not specify *end timing*. We should not allow baseless and unbiblical speculation about the timing of the Second Coming to tempt us into dismissing or discrediting either the fact or the reality of God's glorious future.

There is one passage of Scripture that has been subjected to all sorts of misunderstanding when it comes to end-time issues. It deserves our close attention. The passage is 1 Thessalonians 4:13–5:11. Two divergent claims have been distilled from these verses of Scripture: First, according to some scholars, Paul affirmed that Christ would definitely return in the Apostle's own lifetime. But, so the interpretation goes, clearly Christ didn't return; therefore, Paul was wrong. And since Paul got the timing of the Second Coming wrong, we can dismiss all that he has to say about the future of God's dominion. Second, for other interpreters, Paul affirmed the "rapture" of the church prior to the final tribulation and the return of Christ. (For many interpreters, "rapture" refers to the instantaneous transportation of believers from earth to heaven prior to the second coming of Christ. Unbelievers will remain on earth to endure the Great Tribulation.)

In regard to the first of these claims: Paul uses the metaphor of the "thief in the night" in 1 Thessalonians 5:1-11 to make clear that *no one* knows the timing of Christ's return, not even Paul. Therefore, the believer should be ever vigilant and not be caught by surprise by Christ's return. Second, since Paul didn't know the timing of either the return of Christ or of his own death, he considered it *possible* (but not certain) that Christ may return during his lifetime. Thus when Paul includes himself when he says, "…we who are alive, who are left until the coming of the Lord"

(1 Thessalonians 4:15), we must ask the question: Given the fact that Paul knew neither the timing of Christ's return nor of his own death, what other category than the living could he have used in referring to himself? It would have been ludicrous for him to have said, "…we who will die before the Lord returns." He simply did not know the timing of either of these events. In short, this passage of Scripture does not by any means prove that Paul was convinced that Christ would necessarily come during his own lifetime.

As to the ever-popular issue of the rapture: We need to recognize that theological speculation about the rapture arose only in the nineteenth century. It forms part of a line of thinking known as Dispensationalism, which became popular through the Scofield Reference Bible. There is no historical evidence that the early church believed in the concept of rapture. To the contrary, the early church took texts such as Mark 13:20 to mean that the church would go through the final tribulation while awaiting the second coming of Christ.

The important point to remember is that in speaking about the Second Coming in 1 Thessalonians 4:16-17, Paul is not using the exotic imagery about the rapture. Rather, the Apostle uses an image quite familiar to his audience—the image of the ancient protocol for greeting and welcoming a king and his entourage. (Paul's converts in Thessalonica would have been able to call to mind easily the history of Philip I and Alexander I, who were famous kings of Macedonia, the Roman province in which the city of Thessalonica was located.)

Paul likens the event of Christ's return to the greeting committee that goes out to meet a returning king and to welcome him into the city. This image is much like the entrance liturgy we find in Psalm 24:7-10. The idea is as follows: The king and his entourage are returning to a city. The herald goes before the king blowing a trumpet to alert those on the city walls that the king has arrived and that he should be properly welcomed.

Whereupon the greeting committee departs to meet the king outside the city walls and ushers the king and his entire entourage into the city.

Now, the crucial point for our discussion is this: Paul leaves us hanging, as it were, with the comment: "Then we who are alive, who are left, will be caught up in the clouds together with them to meet the Lord in the air; and so we will be with the Lord forever" (1 Thessalonians 4:17). Paul does not say *where* believers will go once they meet the Lord in the air. Notice, however, that believers are *not* taken up into heaven. Rather, like the royal greeting committee, they will be caught up in the clouds to meet the returning Christ.

Since Paul uses the imagery of a royal return, we may assume that his converts would have deduced that once the believers met the Lord, they would all return with Christ to earth, where he would finish bringing in God's dominion. If this is correct, there is certainly no rapture theology here. First Thessalonians 4:13–5:11, like all other passages of the Bible, must be interpreted in terms of the meaning the first audience of the passage was likely to have given it; it should not be interpreted in light of later Christian theological schemas, of which the early Christians were ignorant.

Conclusion

This chapter has covered a variety of important topics having to do with the future coming of God's dominion. We have dealt with both the fact and the timing of such an event. Perhaps the most important thing I can say about that future coming is that it is in God's hands. This is why we pray for the Dominion to come on earth, rather than simply bringing it about ourselves. In particular, the coming of God's dominion is in the hands of the returning Christ, who will bring it about by overruling the powers of darkness on earth, by raising the dead, and by judging both the living and the dead. This is the process by which God's will, including both justice and mercy, will finally be done on earth as it is in heaven.

Establishing God's final dominion on earth is not a human "program"; rather, it is a divine activity. We will say more about this and the implications following from it in the next chapter.

Questions for Reflection

1 Name some common misunderstandings prevalent today about the future coming of God's dominion, the Second Coming, and the future resurrection of believers.

2 What is heaven, and where is it "located"?

3 What is the difference between "heaven" and the "dominion of God"? Why is this difference important for faith?

4 Why, do you think, are so many Christians today more fascinated with life after death than with the life to come *on earth* when Christ returns?

5 What is the relationship between the promised resurrection of the dead and God's dominion? What does this relationship suggest about the nature of the Dominion on earth?

CHAPTER FIVE

"Thy Will Be Done"

I n Chapter Four we addressed the issue of the future, generally, and the future—the final form—of God's dominion on earth, in particular. That chapter already hinted that not everyone will be included in the final form of God's dominion. Recall, for example, the apostle Paul's subtle warning that only those belonging to Christ will receive a resurrection body like Christ's (1 Corinthians 15:23). Other passages in the New Testament are less subtle. Take Jesus' warning that some people who fully expect to be in God's dominion when it comes in its fullness will be left out (Luke 13:28-30). Or consider an even more ominous passage such as Matthew 13:41-43:

> The Son of Man will send his angels, and they will collect out of his kingdom [dominion] all causes of sin and all evildoers, and they will throw them into the furnace of fire... Then the righteous will shine like the sun in the kingdom [dominion] of their Father.

We could also point to the parables. Consider the parable about the separation of the sheep and the goats (Matthew 25:31-46), which concludes with the words: "And these will go away into eternal punishment, but the righteous into eternal life" (verse 46). Or consider the parable of the wise and foolish bridesmaids, which warns of the dire consequences of failing to be ready for Christ's coming (Matthew 25:1-13).

There is no need to belabor the point. Suffice it to say that the cumulative impression of these biblical passages is clear: Not everyone will be saved, even though God desires that no one should perish.

The consistent witness of the New Testament is that some people have rejected the gospel in the past, others are rejecting it in the present, and yet more will reject the gospel in the future. As a consequence of this rejection, these people will ultimately be lost.

The biblical witness raises in an acute form the issue of final salvation for those who are outside of Christ, for Israel, and indeed for people who are church members but perhaps not true believers. Furthermore, one could ask: If in the end not all people are included in God's dominion, what will be the extent of that dominion? Where else could one be if God's final dominion will extend *throughout* the earth? These are difficult and delicate questions, but they must be raised and discussed if we are to gain clarity about the *scope* of God's saving reign upon the earth and the *final destiny* of everyone within the scope of the divine reign.

As we begin, let us remind ourselves that these issues must be approached with humility and candor, not with arrogance or a judgmental attitude. This is especially so since anyone who is alive is still within the reach of God's grace and of the good news. There is no justification in the New Testament for "writing off" any living soul or any group of people.

The Dominion, Christians, and the Need for Dialogue

Christians, Anti-Semitism, and the Future of Israel

L et's start with the thorny issue of *anti-Semitism,* a term referring to attitudes and acts of discrimination against Jewish people. The issue is important for Christians, because the charge is sometimes made that the New Testament—especially the Gospels of Matthew and John, as well as some of Paul's letters—manifest anti-Semitic ideas.

In many ways, this is an odd charge, not least because Paul himself was a Jew; and, as far as we can tell, the authors of Matthew and John were also Jewish. It would be nearer the mark to say that a number of the authors in the New Testament were engaging in what amounted to an "in-house," prophetic critique of the religion of which they were a part. Recall that the Old Testament prophets were often very strong critics of their own people and their religious practices; and yet no one today would accuse them of anti-Semitism.

The authors of the New Testament are critiquing a *particular form* of early Judaism, not Jews as an ethnic group or Israel as a nation. Specifically, they protested against the people—and the form of early Judaism—who rejected the notion of Jesus as the Jewish Messiah and the savior of the world. In the view of the New Testament writers, true Judaism necessarily includes the recognition of Jesus as the Messiah. For example, Paul's vision of God's people in the new age is that of Jew and Gentile, slave and free, male and female, all united in Christ (Galatians 3:28).

More than any other writer in the New Testament, Paul agonized over the issue of the future of Israel, especially when he saw that the majority of his fellow Jews were rejecting the gospel. Yet even this repeated rejection did not stop Paul from sharing the gospel repeatedly in the synagogues (Acts 13:4-6, 13-52), even at the cost of being punished severely several times for doing so (2 Corinthians 11:24). Nor did the stubborn resistance to Paul's gospel on the part of some Jews cause the Apostle to abandon his people and to stop praying for them or thinking about them. On the contrary, Paul goes so far as to say that he is willing to give up his *own* salvation in Christ for the sake of his people (Romans 9:3)!

Romans 9–11 is an impassioned plea to the largely Gentile congregation of Roman Christians to recognize that God was not finished with the first chosen people, the Jews. Read what Paul says about these non-Christian Jews in Romans 9:4-5:

> They are Israelites, and to them belong the adoption, the glory, the covenants, the giving of the law, the worship, and the promises; to them belong the patriarchs, and from them, according to the flesh, comes the Messiah.

For Paul, this whole matter comes down to whether God is as good as God's word, as good as the divine promises. *God's own character* is at stake in Paul's view; for if God had made many promises (some of them apparently unconditional) to the Jews and then reneged on those promises, on what basis could Gentiles—or anyone else—trust such a capricious God? This is a very good question indeed, and one for which Paul struggles to provide an answer in Romans 9–11.

It is not possible to work through all the complexities of Paul's argument here, but several key points can be made: First, Paul indeed believes that Jesus is the Jewish Messiah. This means that the Apostle believes that God's promises for the Jews are and will be fulfilled; however, these promises find their fulfillment *in Christ*. Paul makes this point very clearly in 2 Corinthians 1:20: "For in him [Christ] every one of God's promises is a 'Yes.' For this reason it is through him that we say the 'Amen' to the glory of God."

Second, Paul says to the Gentile Christians in Rome that God was not caught by surprise when many Jews rejected the good news about Jesus Christ. Because of this rejection, these Jews have been *temporarily* broken off from the people of God. Paul uses the analogy of an olive tree and its branches to make this point (Romans 11:17-23). He stresses, though, that these Jews, if they do not persist in unbelief, can be grafted back into the olive tree (Romans 11:23-24).

Third, Paul believes that a great number of Jews will be grafted back into God's people when Christ returns and the dead are raised. He says this in a variety of ways. In Romans 11:12, Paul speaks of the Jews' eventual full inclusion in Christ. In Romans 11:15, he equates the Jews' acceptance of Christ with "life from the dead" (a possible allusion to the resurrection of the dead). In Romans 11:29, Paul reminds his audience that God's gifts to Israel and the divine call of Israel are irrevocable. In concluding his argument, Paul even says that when Christ returns "all Israel will be saved" (Romans 11:26). By "all Israel" Paul means a very large number of Israelites. God will banish the "ungodliness from Jacob" and will "take away their sins" (Romans 11:26-27); and they will be saved on the same basis as the Gentiles: by grace through faith in Christ.

Fourth, a close reading of Paul's entire argument in Romans 9–11 makes clear his belief that a sovereign God has in fact "broken off" from God's people various olive branches (Jews) in order in the present to graft in, by grace through faith, a variety of wild olive branches (Gentiles). Yet God did this "breaking off" of Jews in order to have mercy on them—that is, to provide an opportunity for them to rejoin the people of God on the basis of grace and faith, rather than on the basis of assumed inheritance rights and the like.

What are the implications of this astounding argument? It means clearly that at no point should Christians "write off" Jews as eternally lost or damned. Some misguided Christians condemn the Jewish people because, in their minds, the Jews are responsible for crucifying Jesus. Such an argument is historically flawed and simply inaccurate. It is true that a distinct minority of Jews—some of the Jewish leaders—had a hand in applying pressure on Pontius Pilate to carry out the Crucifixion; however, in the end, it was the *Romans* who executed Jesus, not the Jews. We would do well to heed Paul's repeated reminder that the final chapter in the story of God's dominion on earth has not yet been written. But when the Dominion is finally complete, among the multitude contained within it will be many Gentiles *and Jews.*

Precisely because the future of Israel is open-ended, we must be careful about the way we speak about dialogue between Jews and Christians. On the one hand, it is clear that we should describe talks between Jews and Christians today as an interfaith dialogue. It is not an ecumenical discussion implying two parties that affirm essentially the same religion. And yet, it is not an interfaith dialogue of the same ilk as, for instance, a discussion between Christians and Buddhists. Jews and Christians share a common scriptural heritage and, to an important extent, a common religious heritage.

The fundamental point of disagreement between Jews and Christians concerns the process of salvation and the role of Jesus in that process. Because of this, there are—and will continue to be—issues about which Christians and their Jewish brothers and sisters will simply have to respectfully agree to disagree. Among these issues are whether the New Testament should be considered part of Holy Scripture, and whether Jews must believe in Jesus in order to be saved.

However, at no point do Christians have the right to say or suggest that God has forsaken the Jewish people or has closed the book on them. Nor should Christianity be seen as the religion that superseded Judaism. To the contrary, for Paul, the faith that he called and proclaimed as the good news was the legitimate and necessary development of the Jewish faith into its proper messianic and final eschatological form.

Christians, Interfaith Dialogue, and the "Scandal of Particularity"

What are the implications of the above discussion for other forms of interfaith dialogue? To begin with, anyone who believes in a God of love—a God who desires that no one should perish—must be open to interfaith dialogue, approaching such conversations with humility. Yet participants in these dialogues should recognize that, at the end of the discussion, differences about the essential beliefs and practices of each faith community will more than likely remain. Indeed, such disagreements happen regularly, unless one of the parties is prepared to give up the distinctive beliefs of its religion. For example, if Moslems were suddenly to affirm the Bible as God's word and reject the Koran— or at least reject their distinctive interpretations of the Bible, of Judaism, and of Christianity—then we might begin to have ecumenical discussions with such a group. But even if this never happened, there are important issues of peace, justice, and love facing us together as a human community. Christians should be able to make common cause with people of other religious traditions around such matters of mutual concern (for example, collaborating on a Habitat for Humanity project or working together to benefit the United Way or Bread for the World). Not only are these causes worth supporting, but they are also a legitimate extension of the gospel. They—and many other causes— deserve our assistance.

Even if Moslems (or any other faith group) did not miraculously accept the Christian gospel, there is still much to be gained from a dialogue that sincerely tries to understand what the differences are between the Christian faith and another religious tradition, and that seeks out areas of agreement, small or large. For me, the essential differences between Judaism and Christianity are less numerous and severe than between

Christianity and other world religions—not least because early Christianity is in many respects an offshoot from early Judaism.

There is indeed a wideness in God's mercy, and the good news is open to *all* people to respond. But God did not promise salvation in advance to all and sundry. There are no promises in Scripture that suggest that a non-Christian group, other than non-Christian Jews, will inevitably be included in the final form of God's dominion.

Sometimes, when discussing the issues of the scope of God's dominion, the nature of salvation, and the purpose of interfaith dialogue, people make reference to the "scandal of particularity." By this phrase they mean the claim by adherents of a particular religious faith that their religion is the *only* means of salvation. Opponents view people who make this sort of claim as arrogant and ignorant, and guilty of unjustifiable religious chauvinism.

The New Testament contains its own scandal of particularity; and I don't think this scandal can be—or for that matter, should be—overcome. The New Testament is unequivocal in its claim that Jesus Christ is God's chosen means of salvation. Yet it is important to remember that *there is a potential universalism within Christian particularity:* All people may be saved through Christ, although it is clear that many have chosen not to avail themselves of this opportunity.

Revelation, Salvation, and God's Character

The issues here are admittedly complex. Consider, for example, the question: Is it possible for God to reveal definitively the divine nature and plan of salvation in *one* particular holy book? Historically and today, the vast majority of Jews, Christians, and Moslems have answered this question with an emphatic yes. God is capable of accurately and adequately revealing the divine will and plan of salvation to humankind.

Yet there are many today who would not view *any* holy book as a revelation from God. Rather, they see these sacred texts as just so many gropings of humankind after God—as a series of inadequate attempts by human beings to formulate their own faith. Such a view, of course, flatly contradicts passages such as 2 Timothy 3:16: "All scripture [in this case, the Old Testament] is inspired by God and is useful for teaching."

Now, if we concede the possibility that a sovereign God is capable of revealing the divine plan accurately and adequately to a particular group of people, the question then becomes: Do we have the right to tell God how that plan must work, or to suggest that God really didn't mean what the Word says God meant? I suggest that we have no such right. A Christian is a person under the authority of God's Word, not the final arbiter over its truth.

In my view, God is perfectly free to create a plan for the salvation of humankind and to execute it as God sees fit. God does not owe salvation to anyone, unless God first promised that salvation to some person or persons. Remember that, according to the New Testament, *all* human beings have sinned and have fallen short of God's best for them. Salvation then becomes not a matter of something *owed to us*, but rather a gift of God's unfailing grace.

This means that whether everyone is saved is not a justice issue; nor is it an issue of the nature of God's character. Rather, it is an issue of *human character* and *human responsibility*. While it is true that many people today would like to live in a no-fault world, the New Testament is quite clear about human beings' moral responsibility for their actions—including the responsibility for how they respond to the gospel.

Revelation, Human Responsibility, and the Extent of Grace

The approach I have taken thus far to the issue of salvation inevitably leads to the question: What about all the people who have never heard the gospel—are they eternally lost just because they have not heard? The answer is no. To answer yes to these questions would indeed raise serious questions about the character of God. It would prompt us to wonder whether we could take seriously the Scripture's testimony that God is love and desires that *no one* perish. In dealing with the issue of the eternal destiny of those who have not heard the gospel, it might be useful to examine a few verses from Romans 1.

Romans 1:18-32 deals directly with the question we have just broached. In these verses, the apostle Paul is speaking of Gentiles who have never heard the gospel. Actually, they have probably never even heard the Hebrew Scriptures read or preached! Nevertheless, Paul says:

> For what can be known about God is plain to them, because God has shown it to them. Ever since the creation of the world his eternal power and divine nature, invisible though they are, have been understood and seen through the things he has made.
>
> (Romans 1:19-20)

Paul is suggesting that the reality and power of the one true God are revealed *in creation.* And since God has created human beings in the divine image, *all* people are capable of understanding this "general revelation." The crucial question is, How will people respond to God's general revelation? Paul goes on in the rest of the chapter to paint a rather bleak picture of repeated negative responses to God's revelation in creation.

The important point to remember, however, is that *no one is condemned for what he or she does not know.* All people are judged in terms of how they respond to the light of salvation they have received. Thus, Paul is able to conclude:

> So they are without excuse; for though they knew God, they did not honor him as God or give thanks to him, but they became futile in their thinking, and their senseless minds were darkened.
>
> (Romans 1:20-21)

God's Will and the Scope of the Dominion

What, then, will be the scope of God's dominion when the climax of history comes? Several thoughts come to mind. First, the Scriptures suggest that ultimately God's dominion will encompass the entire world. Already in the Old Testament we hear promises of the Son of Man having an everlasting Dominion over the earth, and of all peoples and nations serving him (Daniel 7:14).

And yet, even as the author of Revelation describes the beauty of the New Jerusalem and speaks of God and heaven coming down to earth to dwell with humans, he issues this reminder:

> But as for the cowardly, the faithless, the polluted, the murderers, the fornicators, the sorcerers, the idolaters, and all liars, their place will be in the lake that burns with fire and sulfur, which is the second death.
>
> (Revelation 21:8)

Even if we look past the dramatic hyperbole in the author's poetic description of the world's final state, the point is nevertheless made clearly more than once: Not everyone will be saved. Thus when the author describes the New Jerusalem itself, he stresses: "But nothing unclean will enter it, nor anyone who practices abomination or falsehood, but only those who are written in the Lamb's book of life" (Revelation 21:27). This verse implies that some people will be inside the New Jerusalem, and others will be outside.

If it is true that some people will not be included in the New Jerusalem, what are we to make of the promise that *every* knee—whether on earth, in heaven, or under the earth—will eventually bend and every tongue "confess that Jesus Christ is Lord, to the glory of God the Father" (Philippians 2:10-11)?

The point to stress is that in due course, when Christ returns to rule the world, all people will of necessity recognize Jesus for who he is—whether wittingly or unwittingly, willingly or unwillingly.

When it comes to the scope of God's saving work, then, the final issue is not just what a person *knows* about God, but rather what the person *does* with that knowledge. This is borne out, as we have seen, in Paul's discussion both in Romans 1 and in Philippians 2.

Conclusion

In this chapter, we covered a great deal of ground in just a few pages, so it may be well to sum up the implications of our discussion. First, we stressed that although Christ's saving work is *sufficient* for all human beings in every generation, it is only *efficient* (beneficial) for those who accept Christ by faith. Consider the analogy of a person who deposits a million dollars in a bank account and then informs the lucky beneficiary that it's all there for the taking. If the beneficiary does not—or perhaps even refuses—to withdraw the funds, he or she will never be able to enjoy the benefits the money brings. The money does not benefit the person automatically, just by being made available to him or her. The person still has to *do* something about it; he or she has to withdraw the money. Similarly, salvation involves a personal relationship with God through Jesus Christ. That means one must *choose* to be in relationship with God. Only then can one enjoy the benefits of salvation.

Second, we need to take seriously the numerous warnings in Scripture that state that no particular individual or even group of individuals are *automatically* saved. No one automatically enters the future dominion of God; he or she must first *seek* the Dominion, and all other things will be added (Matthew 6:33).

The Scripture passages referred to at the beginning of this chapter warn clearly that it is possible that some people will be eternally lost. The prospect of eternal loss is one reason the early church felt such an urgency to get the word of salvation in Christ out to the world. A God of love does not desire that anyone should perish, but that all should come to a saving knowledge of God. Yet, without the proclamation of the good news, there is no opportunity for a positive response to the gospel of Christ. That is why missions is the essential task of the church if the world is to come to a saving knowledge of Christ.

Third, we spoke about the future of Israel. Romans 9–11 reminds us that God has not gone back on God's promises to the first chosen people. Paul clearly envisions a future in Christ for a large number of Jews who are presently outside of Christ. This means that the church has no business dismissing Jews as if they were eternally lost, any more than Christians should dismiss any group of human beings. Consequently, the New Testament gives no encouragement at all to racism, be it anti-Semitism or any other form of racism.

Fourth, we affirmed the need for Christians to respect the beliefs of other faith groups, even when one must agree to dis-agree about what is essential to the life of faith. Interfaith dialogue can be very helpful. It often helps participants understand more clearly the beliefs and interests they share in common, as well as where the true differences between them lie. When groups discover areas of common interest or concern, they can work together on issues of peace, justice, and love.

Last, from our discussion of Romans 9–11, we learned that the apostle Paul does not affirm the notion that different groups may have different, equally valid, means to God's dominion. Rather, for Paul, the final form of God's dominion consists of one people—whether Jew or Gentile, slave or free, male or female—united *in Christ* (Galatians 3:28).

There is one more issue we must address before we con-clude our study of the dominion of God. We must ask: Is there a future not merely for the earth's inhabitants but for the earth itself? Is animate and inanimate creation doomed to destruction, or will it, too, participate in the renovation of all things when the Dominion comes? This is the topic of the final chapter.

Questions for Reflection

1 How do you respond to the warnings in Scripture that salvation is not automatic but a choice, and that, consequently, some people will not be included when God's dominion is fulfilled?

2 What is the "scandal of particularity"? Do you think the scandal should be done away with in our day? If so, why? If not, why not?

3 Where will the final form of God's dominion take shape, and what is the basis for being included in it?

4. According to this chapter, what is the final destiny of someone who had no knowledge of God's plan of salvation in Christ? Will such a person simply be eternally lost to God?

5 In what ways may Christians benefit from interfaith dialogue? What can you do to foster such dialogues in your community?

CHAPTER SIX

"On Earth as It Is in Heaven"

I n the last two chapters, we discussed at length the future form of God's dominion; however, we concentrated on the *human* dimension of the Dominion, on how the Dominion involves and affects the lives and destiny of human beings.

In this chapter, we introduce another aspect of God's design for the future: the renewal of the earth, of the physical creation itself. If the renewal of all creation is a part of the final form of God's dominion, how would that change the way Christians relate to and treat the earth? This is the kind of question we want to consider in the pages that follow.

The Dominion, Eden, and the New Heaven and Earth

As we mentioned earlier, the New Testament often describes the dominion of God as a *place*—a place that can be entered, obtained, or inherited. If the earth is the place where the fullness of God is going to dwell, then not only must we be a holy people, but also the physical environment that gives us life and supports us will need to be transformed. What would a transformation—a renewal—of the earth mean? What would it involve?

In their images and visions of the end time, the prophets in the Old Testament often likened the future of the earth to its beginnings in the garden of Eden. Consider the following extended quote from Isaiah 65:17-25:

> For I am about to create new heavens
>   and a new earth;
> the former things shall not be remembered
>   or come to mind.
> But be glad and rejoice forever
>   in what I am creating;
> for I am about to create Jerusalem as a joy,
>   and its people as a delight.
> I will rejoice in Jerusalem,
>   and delight in my people;
> no more shall the sound of weeping be heard in it,
>   or the cry of distress.
> No more shall there be in it
>   an infant that lives but a few days,
>   or an old person who does not live out a lifetime;
> for one who dies at a hundred years
>   will be considered a youth,
> and one who falls short of a hundred
>   will be considered accursed.
> They shall build houses and inhabit them;
>   they shall plant vineyards and eat their fruit.
> They shall not build and another inhabit;

they shall not plant and another eat;
for like the days of a tree shall the days of my people be,
   and my chosen shall long enjoy the work of their hands.
They shall not labor in vain,
   or bear children for calamity;
for they shall be offspring blessed by the LORD—
   and their descendants as well.
Before they call I will answer,
   while they are yet speaking I will hear.
The wolf and the lamb shall feed together,
   the lion shall eat straw like the ox;
   but the serpent—its food shall be dust!
They shall not hurt or destroy
   on all my holy mountain,
                says the LORD.

We could easily add to this powerful image the familiar testimony of Isaiah 2:4, which speaks of the time of final judgment:

[God] shall judge between the nations,
and…they shall beat their swords into plowshares,
   and their spears into pruning hooks;
nation shall not lift up sword against nation,
   neither shall they learn war any more.

What is striking about these passages from Isaiah is that both envision a perfectly good, but also perfectly *natural,* new heaven and new earth. Eden, not heaven, is God's desire for us. The first passage, Isaiah 65:17-25, speaks of people living lengthy, blessed lives. Although neither young nor old will die prematurely, interestingly the passage says nothing about the idea of living forever. The passage does say that the animal and human worlds will be at peace, and that this will make it possible for humans to live long and healthy lives. In the prophet's vision, there will be no more human strife; nor will animals prey on one another. *Shalom*—peace and wholeness—will have descended upon the world.

The Dominion and the Freedom of Creation

As beautiful as the prophet Isaiah's vision is, the descriptions in the New Testament of the future Dominion go even further. The apostle Paul, for example, suggests that not only will human strife and the causes of premature death cease, but *death itself* will be eliminated through the resurrection of the dead. Read again 1 Corinthians 15:12-58; also take a look at the discussion of the resurrection of the dead in Chapter Four (pages 58–59).

Other New Testament passages suggest that the earth will be renewed so that those who were raised from the dead may live in an environment suitable to their new holy and blessed condition. Consider, for example, Romans 8:19-24:

> For the creation waits with eager longing for the revealing of the children of God; for the creation was subjected to futility, not of its own will but by the will of the one who subjected it, in hope that the creation itself will be set free from the bondage to decay and will obtain the freedom of the glory of the children of God. We know that the whole creation has been groaning in labor pains until now; and not only the creation, but we ourselves, who have the first fruits of the Spirit, groan inwardly while we wait for adoption, the redemption of our bodies. For in hope we were saved.

The fate of creation and of all its inhabitants is bound up together. When our first parents, Adam and Eve, fell into sin, the effects on us and on the earth were extensive; therefore, we should expect the effects of redemption to be equally extensive.

In the passage quoted above, Paul speaks about God's promise that creation will one day be set free from bondage to decay, and will obtain the same sort of freedom as God's children will at the resurrection. People, made new in the image of Christ, will live in a brand-new world. But the new world will not be just a matter of Eden revisited; rather, it will be Eden as it should have become had Adam and Eve not eaten of the forbidden fruit. Their transgression plunged creation into all kinds of evil, including the evils of disease, decay, and death.

We often hear the stirring words of Revelation 21 read at funerals: The new Jerusalem descends and the voice from the throne says:

> See, the home of God is among mortals. He will dwell with them; they will be his peoples, and God himself will be with them; he will wipe every tear from their eyes. Death will be no more; mourning and crying and pain will be no more, for the first things have passed away.
>
> (Revelation 21:3-4)

If this promise were to come true, it would necessarily involve not just renewed people but also a renewed physical environment—an environment free from disease and decay, struggle and strife. Moreover, since God plans to take up residence with God's people on earth, a new creation is needed, for God is holy and good.

How will this transformation take place? The short answer is this: by means of God's very presence. According to Revelation 22:1-5, "the river of the water of life" flows directly from the presence of God (alluded to by reference to the throne), and this river enlivens and heals all that it touches. It is just the opposite of a polluted and disease-filled river, which defiles all that it touches and all that touch it.

The Dominion and the Redemption of the Earth

The upshot of all this is that God is the ultimate conservationist, the supreme ecologist. This really shouldn't surprise us. After all, God created the world and all that is in it. And afterward, God reveled in what was made, pronouncing it very good (Genesis 1–2).

It is worth remembering that when the Bible speaks of *redemption,* it entails the renewal of the whole creation, not just of human beings. The visions of Revelation 21–22 are not just about a new humanity but about a new creation—a new world.

A moment's reflection will show the wisdom of God's plan to renew the whole creation. Imagine perfected human beings possessing eternal life, and resurrection bodies living in a world full of imperfections, disease, and decay. Imagine redeemed human beings having to spend eternity watching all things bright and beautiful and all creatures great and small continue to decay and die. This scenario could lead only to eternal frustration and sorrow.

There is a good reason why the Bible depicts the new creation as one in which God will wipe away the tears from every eye, and in which there will be no more sorrow or suffering. Eternal life without eternal joy and love and peace would not be the best of all possible worlds. Eternal life without the companionship of the rest of God's creation would not be life in its fullest form. The Bible does not encourage an egocentric view of salvation. Such a view says that redemption is about "saving souls"; it cares little about the ultimate well-being of the material world. But God has much bigger things in mind for creation!

The Dominion and the Coming Feast

The transcending beauty of this whole vision of the future can also be seen in some of Jesus' brief remarks about the messianic banquet. A few examples will suffice.

In Matthew 8:11-12, Jesus says that when the Dominion fully comes, his disciples will join the saints of the Old Testament, such as Abraham and the prophets, in a meal of fellowship (see also Luke 13:28-29). In fact, Jesus said he himself was looking forward to the day (after his death) when he would drink the fruit of the vine anew in the dominion of God (Mark 14:25). The parables of the wise and foolish virgins (Matthew 25:1-13) and of the king planning a wedding feast (Matthew 22:1-14) highlight the future of the Dominion as a feast celebrating the consummation of the union of God and God's people.

Now, to have such a feast, such a lavish banquet, there must be food, and plenty of it. Unless the menu always involves manna from heaven, where would the food come from? From the good earth, of course. Most of the biblical descriptions of the afterlife depict a less ethereal, more concrete vision of what the final future will be for the world and its inhabitants than we sometimes hear about from our pulpits.

Obviously, many of the visions and portrayals of God's final dominion (such as the messianic banquet) come to us as parables and apocalyptic imagery. These forms of literature are more poetry than prose. Consequently, many people are tempted not to take these images very seriously. That would be a mistake; for, as we have seen in Romans 8:19-24, the same sort of ideas about the renewal of creation appear in passages of prose.

What all this suggests to me is this: Through its poetry and its prose, Scripture wants Christians to know that God has a plan for the future of this material world and for God's people—even if we are not meant to take all of the images literally! The purpose of these striking and beautiful images and visions is to portray a future that we can hope for and believe in, a future that will appear when Christ returns and the dominion of God comes fully on earth.

The Dominion and Christian Stewardship

If we were to think of the earth and its future from the perspective of the Dominion, as we have tried to do in this chapter, what would be the implications for the way we live here and now? Let's mention just a few.

First, Christians ought to be diligent in tending and caring for the earth, for in doing so we show others a foretaste of the scope of God's future dominion. All of creation has a purpose and a future in God's design; therefore, we must treat everything in creation with care and respect.

Second, caring for the earth is not merely a sensible short-term strategy, ensuring a decent future for our children and grandchildren. It is also a witness to Christians' conviction that the earth and all that is in it belong to God (Psalm 8). We are not owners of this world; we are only stewards and caretakers of it, for God's sake. The Bible supports neither a godless communistic philosophy nor a godless capitalistic vision for using the world's resources. For Christians, all things belong to God; we are stewards of God's resources. If everything is ultimately God's, then we have an obligation to use and dispose of it in a way that glorifies God and helps humankind.

Such a perspective on stewardship is part of what it means to take seriously the future reign of God upon the earth, for God will hold us accountable for our relationship to the earth. Being held accountable may not be a very pleasurable experience for North Americans, for we tend to be wasteful. We throw away tons of food every day; we support industries that heedlessly pollute rivers and destroy the air; we mistreat our bodies by eating foods that hasten disease, decay, and death.

Third, the function of this discussion is not merely *theological*— to make us aware of what the Bible says about the future of God's dominion. It is also *ethical.* It serves to heighten our sense of responsibility as those who are called to mirror the values of God's dominion.

One way to mirror Dominion values is to become generous with our possessions. After all, they belong to God, not to us. John Wesley, the father of Methodism, has much to teach us about generosity, stewardship, and our attitude toward our possessions. In his oft-preached sermon "The Use of Money," Wesley suggested three "rules" for the responsible stewardship of money: First, make all the money you can; second, save all the money you can; third, give away all the money you can. For Wesley, to make and save all the money you can but not give away as much as you can is to be a living person but a dead Christian![3]

3 See "The Use of Money," a sermon by John Wesley, in *The Works of John Wesley,* Volume VI (Grand Rapids: Zondervan Publishing House, n.d.), pp. 124–36.

Wesley's counsel on money can easily be applied to the stewardship of all our resources, including our use of the earth's resources. Not only does Wesley's view indict our often-excessive and wasteful spending habits, it also reminds us of the responsibility to share our resources with others. After all, we all draw on the same resources of the earth; therefore, no one has the right to hoard or waste these resources. This is particularly true for Christians, who confess that the earth is the *Lord's* (Psalm 24:1).

Once during Easter I served as a Vista aide in the mountains of North Carolina near Burnsville. It was my task to go into the mountains and gather up poor children to take to an Easter egg hunt that had been arranged for them.

I will never forget one particularly poor family, who lived in a shack deep in the mountains. The youngest son, Carl, had never had an opportunity to play with children other than his own siblings. After some persuading, Carl's mother allowed the boy to go with me to the Easter egg hunt. I told her that I would pick Carl up early the next morning.

When I returned the next morning, Carl was waiting for me, with his face scrubbed red so he would look decent. When I got ready to lift Carl into the pickup truck, he handed me an enormous goose egg. The only possession in the world that Carl had was a goose, and he wanted to share its bounty with the other kids at the Easter egg hunt. I learned that day that poverty of the flesh can be adjoined to generosity of the spirit. I learned what stewardship really means: What matters is not how much we have but what we do with what God has given us. Whoever created the bumper sticker that says "He who dies with the most toys wins" surely has never caught a glimpse of God's dominion and its priorities.

The Dominion and Caring for the Whole Creation

The line of thinking in this chapter goes against the grain of the tendency, especially among Western Christians, to interpret the gospel in purely "spiritual" terms. Turning God's dominion into an exclusively spiritual reality shields Christians from having to deal with the implications of God's Word for our material realities. But, as we have seen, God's reign extends over body and spirit, the invisible and visible realms, heaven and earth. Therefore, to divide our reality into the spiritual and the material realms, and then to care only about the spiritual realm, is unjustified. Indeed, it is a cop-out meant to help us justify the irresponsible ways in which we often handle the material world.

The gospel is about the salvation of the whole person. Furthermore, there are even incursions of miraculous healing in the here and now; this is God's way of saying that God has not given up on embodied existence. If the dominion of God is indeed coming to earth in the future and there will be an accounting for what we have done on this planet, it behooves us to recognize the implications of the *whole* gospel for *every* aspect of life here and now. The Dominion has a claim on it all.

Conclusion

It is my hope that through this study you have gained a larger vision of the nature, extent, place, and timing of God's saving reign, so that you will be able to pray more adequately, "Thy kingdom come," and that you will be prepared for that reality in God's own good time.

It is hoped that you will also now recognize that God's dominion exists already in our lives and should be celebrated, shared, and acted upon. To an extent, the good news of the gospel is, "The future is now." And to an extent, that same good news announces, "The future is not yet."

As we live in anticipation between the time of the first and second advents of Christ, let us ponder the implications of the issues raised in the book; and let us then truly live as bearers of God's dominion.

Questions for Reflection

1 According to the Bible, what is the future of the earth in God's plan of salvation?

2 This chapter suggests that the dominion of God is neither spiritual nor material, but both. What does this mean for the way we relate to and treat the earth?

3 This chapter refers to God as the ultimate conservationist or ecologist. Do you agree with that portrayal of God? Why? Why not?

4 In what ways is God's plan to renew the creation an incentive for stewardship?

5 What can you do, both in your personal lifestyle and in your community, to care for creation? How would such caring be a reflection of God's dominion?

Celebrating the Dominion in Kingdomtide

T he season of Kingdomtide deserves greater emphasis in United Methodist congregations. This season, also known as Ordinary Time or the season after Pentecost, starts the day following Pentecost and ends the day before the First Sunday of Advent. Referring to this season as Kingdomtide allows United Methodists to focus on the theme of God's dominion and reign. (See *The United Methodist Book of Worship*, page 409, for more information about Kingdomtide.)

One way to place greater emphasis on the season of Kingdomtide is for clergy to preach on the subject of the Kingdom (Dominion) during the season of Kingdomtide.

A second way to foster greater awareness of Kingdomtide is to use *The Realm of the Reign* as a small-group study, either in Sunday school or at another appropriate time. The book can easily be taught in seven sessions in as many weeks during Kingdomtide (one session for the introduction and one session for each of the six chapters).

A third way for churches to emphasize Kingdomtide is to develop rituals suitable for Kingdomtide, as we have done for other liturgical seasons. Why not draw on the ceremonies we already have for celebrating Thanksgiving and incorporate these during Kingdomtide into our reflection on the coming of God's dominion on earth? Thanksgiving is a particularly appropriate time to reflect on the messianic banquet, on the goodness of the earth, on our responsibility to care for the earth, and on the new heaven and new earth God has promised. Thanksgiving images of harvest and harvest home coincide nicely with the images of the future messianic reign upon the earth and the fellowship it will entail.

In addition, some rituals of *renewal* would also be appropriate during the season of Kingdomtide. Perhaps we could develop a ritual for the consecration of a new home built through Habitat for Humanity. Or we could use a ritual to celebrate our congregation's effort to clean up a stream or pick up garbage in a park or along a roadside. Rituals that help us hallow all of life are worth creating; they provide a visible symbol of the message of Kingdomtide.

Last, Kingdomtide is an especially appropriate time for prayer and fasting, and for collecting goods and funds for the less fortunate. The Lord's Prayer and its various petitions are also apt subjects for study or proclamation during Kingdomtide.